Our universe is incredible.

Let the LEGO minifigures share it with you.

And check out the epic building ideas.

Ahoy, matey! There's a treasure chest of facts inside ready to open.

A scientific fact: this book is fun!

Factastic!

Polly want a fact? There are dozens to explore and learn.

Awesome minifigures like me will show you around and make you hippie ... I mean, happy.

ISS astronauts orbit the Earth about 16 times every day. They have given us truly amazing pictures of planet Earth.

AURORA BOREALIS

American astronaut Scott Kelly filmed this incredible view of the Aurora Borealis from the International Space Station (ISS). Streams of colour shimmer across the sky above the North Pole when electrically charged particles from the Sun strike atoms and molecules in Earth's atmosphere and cause them to light up.

CONTENTS

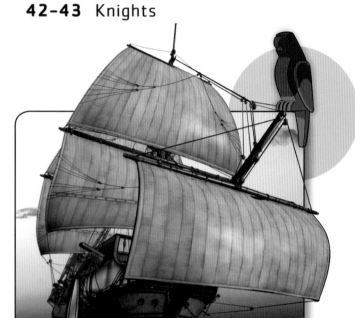

Meet the Romans on page 22. We ruled the world for 500 years.

Find out which Native American inventions you use every day on page 34.

Fantastic facts pop up everywhere!

Bats can find food in total darkness. Hang out with us underground on page 94.

Right now, there are 2,000 thunderstorms on Earth. Read up on page 70.

Eureka! Just 92 elements make everything on Earth. Learn more on page 58.

Greet the geeks on page 104.

We're searching the universe to find new planets.

You don't say! We're searching the universe for intelligent life. Better read this book.

Beep beep!

Learning makes everyone a winner.

No clowning around. At the end of this book, you'll be filled with facts.

IT'S HISTORY

Step back in time with the LEGO® minifigures as they reveal how history was made. Meet some amazing people from the past who built pyramids, ruled empires, wore blingy crowns, sailed the world AND liked chocolate.

All this happened back then to make the world what it is today. Guess what's next?

CAVE PEOPLE

Me Caveman. Me a rock star.

Early – or prehistoric – humans lived in caves, hunted with clubs and stones, and liked to dabble in art. They had tough lives, especially since their neighbours were sabre-toothed tigers! But their brains were large – and growing larger. Humans would have a great future.

The most important thing we did was discover fire.

MEET LUCY

This fossilized skeleton found in Ethiopia (and named Lucy) is about 3 million years old. It is the most ancient early human skeleton that has ever been found.

MINI PICS

What did you do today?

Oh, I smashed some rocks to make tools.

Then I made some new clothes with this animal skin. Oh, and built some animal traps. You?

I went clubbing.

WHAT'S FOR DINNER?

Scientists study prehistoric teeth to figure out what people ate. It turns out they munched on just about anything. Nuts, seeds, grasses, ferns, bugs, fruits, animal guts and birds' eggs were all on the menu. They even ate papyrus (a tough plant later used to make paper) – so they might have eaten the menu, too!

2,500,000– 1,400,000 BCE
The first knives appeared. They were really just rock flakes.

1,000,000 BCE
Use of fire – awesome! It was much easier to keep warm, cook and work at night.

500,000–100,000 BCE
The first fashion – fur, leather, leaves and grass were draped or tied around the body.

Many early artists left their handprints on cave walls. A handy way to sign their art, perhaps?

Me have facts ON head. Need IN head.

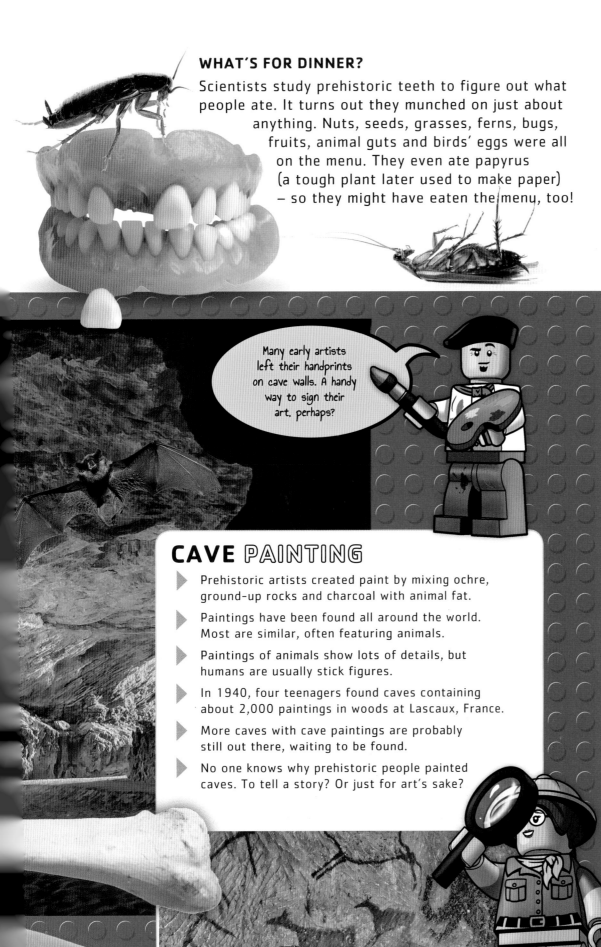

CAVE PAINTING

▶ Prehistoric artists created paint by mixing ochre, ground-up rocks and charcoal with animal fat.

▶ Paintings have been found all around the world. Most are similar, often featuring animals.

▶ Paintings of animals show lots of details, but humans are usually stick figures.

▶ In 1940, four teenagers found caves containing about 2,000 paintings in woods at Lascaux, France.

▶ More caves with cave paintings are probably still out there, waiting to be found.

▶ No one knows why prehistoric people painted caves. To tell a story? Or just for art's sake?

60,000 BCE
Island-hopping people in Southeast Asia made boats from logs.

30,000 BCE
Flutes made of mammoth tusks – music as well as art. Things were looking up!

3500 BCE
Wheels! They made moving heavy loads wheel-y much easier.

Would you look at that? Cattle, birds, bears, cats and even rhinos appeared on cave walls.

ANCIENT EGYPT

In about 3000 BCE, most people in the world were still living in caves and hitting each other over the head with clubs. Not in Egypt! Ancient Egyptians were busy writing, feasting, inventing, farming, boating, trading, conquering and building pyramids. They were a truly awe-inspiring ancient civilization.

DESERT RIVER

Egypt would be a massive sand bowl in the northern Sahara desert if not for the Nile River. It floods every year, leaving behind a fertile valley. This flooding made the ancient Egyptians rich in food and water. About 95% of Egyptians today still live on the banks of the Nile.

GODS AND CATS

Ancient Egyptians worshipped more than 2,000 different gods and goddesses. One of them was the protective goddess Bastet, who was half cat and half woman – the original Catwoman! Cats were favoured animals in ancient Egypt, so much so that they were considered sacred.

How many blocks in the Great Pyramid? More than 2 million! Awesome.

FANTASTIC PHARAOHS

Pharaohs ruled in ancient Egypt. They were worshipped as gods, and everything they said was made law. The pharaoh ran the empire, built temples and planned the afterlife. No one was allowed to touch him, and people had to bow down on the floor upon meeting him.

BUILD IT!

BUILD A GOLD COFFIN (SARCOPHAGUS) AND SURROUND IT WITH

HIEROGLYPHS

Ancient Egyptians called their picture writing *medu netjer*, meaning "words of God". But it was the ancient Greek name that stuck: *hieroglyph*, or "sacred carving".

IT'S A WONDER

Towering above the desert sands, the pyramids at Giza are one of the world's architectural wonders. More than 4,500 years old, they were built as tombs for the ancient Egyptian pharaohs.

The Great Pyramid of Giza was 3,675 LEGO® Minifigures high! That's 147 m (482 ft) tall.

The Egyptians preserved, or mummified, the bodies of their dead so they would remain lifelike.

I'm the first wrap star!

MORE TREASURE!

The discovery of King Tut's tomb caused a sensation! The whole world went CRAZY for everything Egyptian.

Ancient Egyptians believed that they needed their stuff to enjoy the afterlife. So they filled their tombs with treasures and goodies. They preserved their bodies as mummies, wrapped in bandages. Tomb-builders added secret rooms to keep everything hidden. King Tutankhamen's mummy wasn't discovered until 1922, by British archaeologist Howard Carter.

KING TUT'S TOMB TREASURES

2 thrones

A golden mask

A solid gold coffin

Food and 30 jars of wine

Perfumes, oils and ointments

Clothing made of the finest linen

Rings, necklaces and other jewellery

Golden and jewelled chests full of treasure

Sandals with images of King Tut's enemies

139 ebony, ivory, silver and gold walking sticks

MYSTIFYING
MUMMIES OF EGYPT

1. An Egyptian mummy was found with its tongue sticking out!

2. The mummy of Egyptian princess Henuttawy was packed so full that she burst her bandages.

3. Over 300,000 mummified cats were found at the temple to the Egyptian goddess Bastet.

4. One Egyptian mummy was found with two left legs!

5. Some mummies were completely covered by a thin layer of gold.

6. 3,000-year-old mummies have been found with hair and skin.

7. It took 70 days to make a mummy.

8. Here's an eye-opening fact: Pharaoh Ramses IV's mummy had fake eyeballs made from a pair of onions.

9. Many royal mummies have their arms crossed high on their chests.

10. Pharaoh Tutankhamen had a necklace made from glass produced by a meteor impact.

11. People in Victorian England would buy tickets to watch mummies being unwrapped.

12. Mummified snakes, shrews, birds, monkeys and crocodiles have all been found.

Come on, mummy. We've all paid to see you unwrapped...

It's going to take a while. Those bandages can be a mile long!

Arggh! I doubt I'm going to look that pretty!

Shhh!

FIVE MONSTER MYTHS FROM ANCIENT GREECE

Ancient Greek civilization lasted from the 8th century BCE until 146 BCE. Greek culture has had a huge influence on the world. Greek myths are the starting point for many world-famous stories. They tell of powerful gods and human heroes battling terrible monsters.

HERCULES

Hercules was the son of Zeus and a mortal woman. He angered the gods and was challenged to 12 tasks. He had to defeat many monsters, such as the Nemean lion and the deadly Stymphalian birds. The ferocious hydra, a nine-headed snake, almost got the better of him.

MEDUSA

Medusa was a beautiful human girl who greatly upset the goddess Athena. Her hair was turned into snakes and her face became so terrible that anyone she looked at turned to stone. The hero Perseus defeated Medusa, and from her body sprang Pegasus, the winged horse.

SIRENS

The Sirens were part birds, part beautiful women who lured sailors to shipwreck with their enchanting songs. The hero Odysseus told his ship's crew to tie him to the mast so he could listen to the Sirens' song, though it almost drove him mad.

Many creatures in Greek myths were half human, half animal. I'm a faun - half man, half goat!

CYCLOPS

Polyphemus was a cyclops, a one-eyed giant. He shut the hero Odysseus in a cave. Polyphemus asked his name and Odysseus replied, "Nobody." Odysseus attacked him and escaped. The cyclops shouted, "Nobody hurt me."

MINOTAUR

The Minotaur had the head of a bull and the body of a man. King Minos built a huge labyrinth to keep him in. No one could find their way through the maze. The hero Theseus managed to navigate the paths, unravelling thread as he went. He defeated the Minotaur, then followed the wool back again.

Brave and powerful Hercules was the greatest of all Greek heroes!

Odysseus was greater! He defeated a bunch of monsters on his way home from the Trojan War. Including you!

GREAT ROMAN EMPERORS

Julius Caesar was a general who wanted total power. He died in 44 BCE, but the rise of the emperors had begun.

Augustus became the first emperor in 31 BCE. He built up the army, roads and Rome's forum or central square.

Trajan ruled from 98 CE. He made the empire bigger and much richer and put up some amazing buildings.

BUILD IT!

BUILD A GLADIATORS' ARENA, COMPLETE WITH ARCHES TO MAKE

ANCIENT ROME

Rome was the capital city of a mighty empire lasting around 500 years from 31 BCE until 476 CE. On the one hand, its citizens enjoyed fancy public baths, strolls in the forum, stone newspapers and great roads. On the other hand, they watched gladiators fight for entertainment ... and had some crazy emperors!

THE COLOSSEUM

Up to 55,000 Roman spectators flocked through the 80 arches of the Colosseum to be entertained for the night. One favourite show was watching armed and highly trained gladiators fight. Some gladiators were slaves forced to fight. Others were desperate for prize money and glory.

Gladiators were celebrities. Kids even made gladiator action figures from clay.

NOT SO GREAT

Nero (54 CE) was blamed for a huge fire that destroyed much of Rome. When he rebuilt, he took a huge plot of land for himself.

Commodus (180 CE) fancied himself as a tough gladiator. Of course, he cheated to make sure that he won!

Caligula (37 CE) declared war on a seashore and ordered soldiers to gather shells! He tried to give his horse a top job.

AN ENTRANCE.

THE VIKINGS

They came from Sweden, Denmark and Norway and sailed, traded and raided all over Europe between 700 and 1100. The Vikings were known as fearsome warriors, but they were also bold explorers, peaceful farmers and they had a wonderful culture filled with legends and music.

LONGBOAT CONSTRUCTION

Vikings sailed the seas in longboats. These shallow ships were ideal for sailing rough seas and slipping through narrow harbours. They navigated by looking for landmarks, such as islands and distant mountains, and by watching birds and whales.

1 The keel
A longboat's keel (bottom) was carved, then held in place with wooden blocks.

2 The sides
Overlapping planks were carefully nailed together to make the sides of the boat.

3 The prow
A dragon's head was carved on the boat's prow (front). It often glinted with gold.

4 The mast
The mast was raised. Stones were added to keep the ship as stable as possible.

About 80 trees are needed to build a longboat. I'd better get chopping!

MINI PICS

I, Leif Eriksson, son of Erik the Red, hereby claim this land.

Grrr. We already live here.

I hoped for a welcome party.

I can give you a bear hug!

BUILD IT!

DESIGN A VIKING LONGBOAT, COMPLETE WITH A FANTASTIC

VIKING VILLAGES

Some Vikings spent many years at sea. Others settled abroad, marrying locals and setting up villages. There are Viking descendants in many parts of the world.

He only popped out for a loaf of bread and he's been gone eight years.

5 **A single square**

Finally, the sail was unfurled. Oarsmen had to bring their own trunks to sit on!

VIKING LEGENDS

The Vikings told many stories about gods, giants, trolls and dragons. They were full of magic, adventure, trickery and mischief. They described gods and goddesses living in a sky-world called Asgard, and people living in Midgard (Middle-Earth). A rainbow bridge linked Midgard with Asgard.

MAGICAL RUNESTONES

Vikings carved symbols, drawings and letters called runes on to stones. These runestones marked property or told the tale of a big event.

I will become famous! The first person from Europe to reach this new land!

I can't bear it. Time for you to Leif!

Vikings had style. They took baths (usually on Saturdays), carried combs and bleached their hair.

BARK, BUG and DIRT are Viking words!

ANIMAL'S HEAD ON THE BOAT'S PROW. SAIL ON!

ANCIENT CHINA

China was home to one of the most impressive civilizations of all time. Over thousands of years, the ancient Chinese developed a rich culture, dozens of amazing inventions and one incredible wall!

Kung Fu is as old as China itself. People were often at war and needed to defend themselves. Hai-ya!

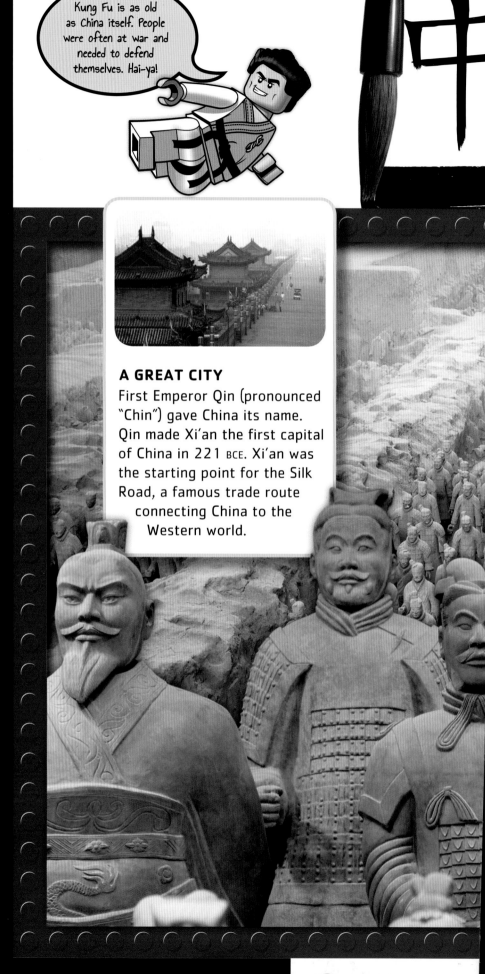

WORLD-FAMOUS WALL

To keep out their great enemies, the ancient Chinese built a great wall. The Great Wall snakes across mountains, deserts and grasslands for 21,196 km (13,170 miles). It took 2,000 years to build, starting in 221 BCE.

TOP 10 GREAT CHINESE INVENTIONS

1. Printing press
2. Fireworks
3. Clocks
4. Compasses
5. Kites
6. Wheelbarrows
7. Paper
8. Silk-making
9. Football
10. Tea

A GREAT CITY

First Emperor Qin (pronounced "Chin") gave China its name. Qin made Xi'an the first capital of China in 221 BCE. Xi'an was the starting point for the Silk Road, a famous trade route connecting China to the Western world.

BUILD IT

国

Mandarin is the official form of Chinese. *Ni hao* means "hello!" *Ni hao ma* means "How are you?"

Shhh!

CHARACTER BUILDING

Chinese characters first appeared as symbols and pictures carved on to animal bones more than 3,000 years ago. These have evolved into the modern Chinese characters.

Colours have meaning in China. Red represents happiness and prosperity. Yellow is lucky.

TIME LINE

QIN'S TERRACOTTA ARMY

Qin ordered the creation of an entire army of clay statues to guard his tomb and show off his power. Some 720,000 craftsmen worked on the enormous army of eight thousand life-size horsemen, archers and soldiers.

8000–2205 BCE
Early Chinese settlers built villages.

2205–1574 BCE
The Xia became the first dynasty.

551 BCE
Confucius was born. This great philosopher helped shape Chinese society.

Confucius said, "Wherever you go, go with all your heart!"

The army was buried for 2,000 years before farmers digging a well found it. Well, what a surprise!

221 BCE
Qin Shi Huangdi linked existing walls to build the Great Wall.

210 BCE
Emperor Qin died and was buried with his Terracotta Army.

1368–1644
The Ming dynasty ruled. The Forbidden City was begun and it was a time of great cultural progress.

Women sometimes trained and fought alongside male samurai.

THE WAY OF THE WARRIOR
For more than 700 years, shoguns ruled ancient Japan, supreme commanders of the elite warriors, the samurai. The samurai came to follow a code called the *bushido* or "way of the warrior". Fierce loyalty was all-important but also learning, good behaviour and not being concerned with material things. Here samurai general Minamoto Yoshitsune dictates a letter to the shogun to ask for his forgiveness after losing a battle.

ROYAL RULERS

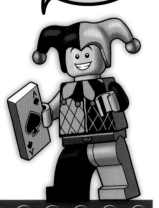

History has seen some all-powerful kings, queens and emperors. There have been good, bad and really rotten rulers, with splendid palaces and courts full of colourful characters. Even now, in Europe, there are 10 reigning royal families. Queen Elizabeth II is the queen of 16 countries!

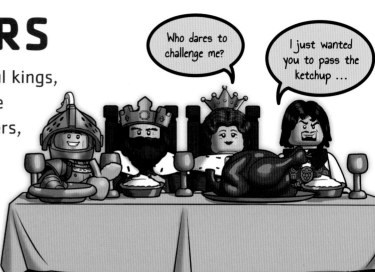

Who dares to challenge me?

I just wanted you to pass the ketchup ...

TOP ROYAL PALACES

Buckingham Palace, England
Principal home of Elizabeth II.

Pena National Palace, Portugal
Built high in the Sintra mountains.

Mysore Palace, India
Built by the local royal family, the Wodeyars.

Forbidden City, China
Home to Chinese emperors for about 500 years.

Palace of Versailles, France
Fantastic home of the Sun King, Louis XIV.

Amalienborg
Home to the Danish royal family – has four identical buildings.

Grand Palace Bangkok
One of the most popuar tourist attractions in Thailand.

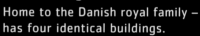

Neuschwanstein Castle
A fairy-tale castle built by a shy king of Bavaria in the 19th century.

  BUILD IT!   **BUILD A SPECTACULAR ROYAL PALACE FOR A QUEEN OR KING.**

Suleiman I (ruled 1520–1566) Suleiman led the Ottoman Empire of modern-day Turkey to the height of its power. Known as fair and wise, he was an epic poet.

Elizabeth I (ruled 1559–1603) Only the third queen of England to rule in her own right. Elizabeth forged a strong nation with a flourishing culture.

Gustav II Adolf (ruled 1611–1632) Nicknamed "the lion of the North", Gustav was a military genius who made Sweden into a modern power.

King Louis XIV (ruled 1643–1715) Known as the Sun King, Louis was King of France for 72 years. France became the most successful country in Europe.

Peter the Great (ruled 1682–1725) Known as the Tsar, Peter changed Russian life, from creating a tech-savvy navy to founding St Petersburg.

INCREDIBLE CROWN

The Imperial State Crown belongs to Elizabeth II. It has over 3,000 gems, including a 317-carat diamond. To get the diamond to London, detectives pretended it was on a steamboat while really sending it as a parcel in a plain box.

In 1845, the Imperial State Crown fell off a cushion and broke! The gems were put in a new setting in 1937.

ETIQUETTE

Etiquette, or social rules, was very important in royal courts. French King Louis XIV had very strict codes – not following them was a crime! To stay on a king's good side, follow these simple rules:

1. Never knock on the king's door – just gently scratch.

But scratching will ruin my manicure!

2. Always address the king as "Your Royal Highness".

Whoops! I called him Your Disloyal Slyness!

3. Never cross your legs in public.

Cross my legs? You've got to be kidding!

4. A lady must never hold hands with a gentleman.

He's no gentleman!

5. Never turn your back on someone of higher status!

How dare you show your back! Come back!

I'm scared to turn back …

6. When the king wakes, everyone must be fully dressed.

Lie-ins are dangerous. Hide me, Teddy!

AZTECS AND INCAS

Two incredible empires dominated Central and South America between the 13th and 16th centuries, though they never met. Some of their most beautiful buildings and fantastic treasures can still be seen today. Best of all, the Aztecs were big hot-chocolate drinkers and ate corn tortillas with everything!

QUETZALCOATL
The god of knowledge and learning.

THE AZTECS

Tenochtitlan (now Mexico City) was the heart of the Aztec Empire. The Aztecs were great warriors. Every boy trained to be a soldier. They wore animal helmets, like this eagle, to show rank.

GREAT PYRAMIDS

The Aztecs worshipped around 200 gods. They built tall pyramids to honour them that reached to the skies. The Acatitlan temple was dedicated to the gods of the Sun and the rain.

Argghh! Hot chilli with chocolate! That's no treat!

Nobody ate chocolate back then, they only drank it.

OLD **HOT** CHOCOLATE

The cacao tree grows in the rainforest of Central America. Chocolate comes from its seeds. The Aztec emperor Montezuma II drank 50 cups a day!

MONTEZUMA'S BREW

1. Cacao beans were roasted and ground to a paste. 2. Water and maize flour were added. 3. Vanilla and really HOT CHILLI PEPPERS were added. 4. The drink was poured back and forth from cup to pot until frothy!

OLD T

GODS AND GODDESSES

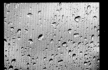

TLALOC
The rain god.

TONATIUH
The god of the Sun.

CENTEOTL
Goddess of maize, the most important food.

CHALCHIUHTLICUE
Goddess of water and all aquatic elements.

THE INCAS

The great Inca Empire thrived in the snow-capped Andes mountain range. Machu Picchu was an estate built for an emperor in Peru. The ruins are so remote that it was not discovered by Europeans until the 20th century. There were houses, temples and terraces for growing food.

The Inca emperor Atahualpa had a throne of solid gold. He was sitting on a gold mine!

THE END OF THE EMPIRES

By the end of the 15th century, stories of cities of gold spread through Europe. The conquistadors from Spain and Portugal set out to claim the riches. They defeated the Aztec and Inca Empires and took over the whole of Central and South America.

TIME LINE

1200
In South America, tribes across the Andes Mountains unite under a ruler called the Inca.

1325
In Central America, the Aztecs build the city of Tenochtitlan in the middle of a lake.

1438
The ruling Inca, Pachacuti Yupanqui, begins conquests that lead to a mighty empire.

1440
Montezuma I leads the Aztecs, expanding their empire across Central America.

Young Aztecs became warriors at the age of 17.

1450
Machu Picchu is built. The Inca Empire now stretches 2,000 miles down the Pacific Coast.

1519
The Spanish conquistador, Hernán Cortés, arrives in Tenochtitlan. By 1522 he has defeated the Aztecs.

1532
The conquistador Pizarro and his army defeat the Inca Empire (but they missed Machu Picchu!)

FIVE AWESOME THINGS FROM THE
NATIVE AMERICANS

KAYAKS

The Inuit people of the Arctic were using kayaks from around 4,000 years ago. Early kayaks were made of driftwood. They were one-person boats designed to stay afloat in rough water.

People have lived in the Americas for thousands of years, from the freezing Arctic, through the Great Plains of the United States, all the way to the rainforests of South America. Native American cultures have introduced a host of things that are used right around the world, every day.

TOBOGGANS

The native people of northern Canada built a *nobugidaban* – a word meaning "flat" and "drag". We call it a toboggan. *Nobugidabans* were made from slats of wood bent into a shape like the letter *J*.

LACROSSE

Lacrosse was one of the many varieties of stick and ball games played by Native Americans, especially in the eastern part of North America. It was played with a ball, which was caught with curved rackets with a net on one end. The stick used by the Iroquois people is the one that we use today.

TEPEE

Native Americans of the Great Plains moved around a lot in search of food, so they needed portable houses. They built cone-shaped tents called tepees. These were warm and dry in winter and cool in the summer, and among the first mobile homes.

POPCORN

10,000 years ago, the South Americans grew a type of corn that exploded into a delicious snack. They have been popping corn ever since! The Aztecs used popcorn to adorn their headdresses and as an offering to their god of corn.

When you next wrap up in a warm ski jacket, think of an Inuit! They fashioned parkas by using lots of layers to trap warm air.

Native Americans wore some super-comfortable moccasins.

There are seven rays on Lady Liberty's crown, one for each of the seven continents of the world.

STATUE OF LIBERTY

A statue called *Liberty Enlightening the World* was a gift of friendship from France to the United States. The French sculptor Frédéric-Auguste Bartholdi designed the statue with the help of Gustave Eiffel, designer of the Eiffel Tower in Paris. Liberty arrived in New York harbour in 1885. She stands near Ellis Island, the gateway to America for millions of immigrants in the first half of the 20th century. She is the world's largest copper statue, 34 m (111 ft 6 in) from heel to head.

Ready for a good knight? See page 42.

Meet some of the boldest battlers ever on page 40.

I'm off to discover something on page 44.

HEROES

We've found out some factastic facts from history. Now let's meet some of the most colourful characters who made all that history happen. Let the LEGO®

Shiver your timbers on page 46.

Gallop on over to page 50, cowpoke. Yee-hah!

AND VILLAINS

minifigures show you who's who. You'll encounter mighty warriors, brave and loyal knights, dashing explorers, particularly peg-legged pirates and cowboys at home on the range. They found a place in the history books, and in this one, too.

Go, go, Caesar! He's our leader!

MIGHTY WARRIORS

Who's the most fearsome fighter ever? Read on to find out more about history's great warriors. They built empires and battled bravely. Some even rode elephants.

JULIUS CAESAR

c.100–44 BCE

Home: Rome, Italy

Skills: A strong leader, skilled negotiator and great with battlefield strategy

Bio: Julius Caesar was a Roman general whose victories expanded Rome's empire, including modern-day France and Belgium. He knew the name of everyone who fought for him, which made him a popular leader.

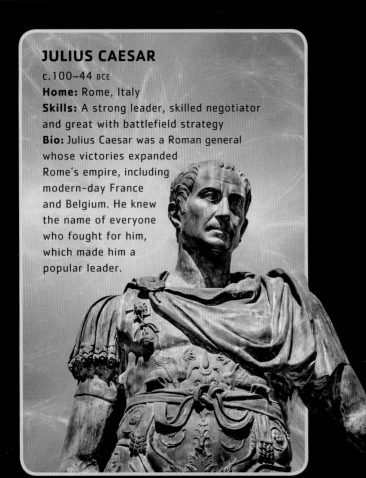

ALEXANDER THE GREAT

356–323 BCE

Home: Pella, Macedonia

Skills: Ambitious, a smart thinker and a skilled politician with a big imagination

Bio: Alexander the Great became king of Macedonia when he was only 19. He built a massive empire that stretched from Greece to India.

TIMUR (AKA TAMERLANE)

1336–1405

Home: Samarkand, Uzbekistan

Skills: Brave, smart and clever with battlefield strategy

Bio: Timur was one of the greatest warriors of Eurasia (where Europe and Asia meet). He conquered lands from Turkey to India, and also loved art and culture.

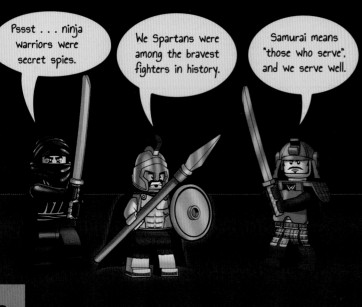

Pssst . . . ninja warriors were secret spies.

We Spartans were among the bravest fighters in history.

Samurai means "those who serve", and we serve well.

All hail, Caesar! I came, I saw, I conquered.

Round one! Who is the mightiest of them all?

VENI, VIDI, VICI

1. UNITED THE TRIBES OF MONGOLIA 2. BROUGHT CHINESE MEDICINE AND DOCTORS TO HIS PEOPLE 3. CREATED AN EARLY POSTAL SYSTEM TO SEND MESSAGES ACROSS HUGE AREAS 4. HELPED OPEN UP THE EAST TO THE WEST

Genghis Khan, he's our man!

BOUDICCA

died 60 CE
Home: Norfolk, England
Skills: Courage and bravery
Bio: A famous female warrior and queen of the Iceni tribe. When the Roman Empire was in charge in England, Boudicca led her people in a rebellion against it. She was defeated, but her bravery lived on in legend.

HANNIBAL

247–183 BCE
Home: Carthage (present-day Tunisia)
Skills: Resourcefulness and elephant-riding
Bio: Hannibal started a war with the Roman Empire at the age of 26. He eventually advanced towards Rome, crossing the Alps with a herd of elephants.

ATTILA THE HUN

c. 406–453
Home: Pannonia (present-day Hungary)
Skills: Fierce and ruthless
Bio: Attila conquered a chunk of the Roman Empire from the Black Sea to the Mediterranean. His fearsome nickname was Flagellum Dei ("Scourge of God").

GENGHIS KHAN

c. 1162–c. 1227
Home: Lake Baikal, Mongolia
Skills: Strategy, spying, hands-free horse-riding
Bio: Founder and Great Khan of the Mongol Empire. Genghis conquered much of northeast Asia and China. He ruled over the largest empire the world has ever seen.

Sorry, Caesar. There's none like the Hun.

Boudicca was a warrior woman, too!

I wish I had a fearsome nickname.

These warriors became legends in their lifetimes.

KNIGHTS

The Middle Ages in Europe was the period from about 1000 to 1500. All-powerful kings granted lands to their loyal lords, who built towering castles. The lords employed armies of brave knights to defend their castles and fight for king and country.

I challenge you to a fight, knight!

Ugh, knights could never refuse to fight or they would be dishonoured.

I have a joke for you, brave knight. What do knights wear to bed?

Err ... knighties?

A KNIGHT IN SHINING ARMOUR

In the Middle Ages, a suit of armour entirely encased a knight's body, like a portable fortress. The full suit weighed as much as a 7-year-old child.

HOW TO BECOME A KNIGHT

▶ It was expensive. The first step in becoming a knight in the Middle Ages was to be born into a wealthy and noble family.

▶ At age 7, a boy became a page, which was a bit like going to school. He learnt to read, write and use a bow and arrow.

▶ At 14, a page became a squire and worked for a knight. He cleaned armour, helped the knight dress for battle and learned to fight.

▶ The day before he turned 21, a squire was given a freezing-cold bath. The next day he was knocked on the head with his sword by his lord.

▶ The knight could now be called "Sir".

COATS OF ARMS

In the confused combat of a battlefield, it was difficult to work out who was who. Each knight had a specially designed coat of arms that he wore on his shield or tunic. Messengers called heralds could recognize every coat of arms so they could pass on instructions.

Knights were the only soldiers who rode horses, called destriers, on the battlefield.

THE TOURNAMENT

Between battles, knights had to keep their skills sharp. They did this by taking part in tournaments. Knights would take turns fighting one-on-one. The winner would sometimes take the loser's weapons or even his horse!

The most popular event at a tournament was the joust.

SUPERSTAR EXPLORERS' ADVENTURES

1. In 629, Chinese Buddhist monk Xuanzang takes an epic road trip to India to check if the Buddhist writings he had were right. It takes him 16 years.

2. In 1325, Muslim explorer Ibn Battuta begins his 121,000-km (75,000-mile), 30-year journey by foot and camel around Africa and Asia.

3. In 1492, Christopher Columbus is the first European to set foot in the Americas since the Vikings in 1000.

4. In 1557, the galleon the *Golden Hind* set sail on its round-the-world voyage. Its captain is England's Sir Francis Drake.

5. In 1804, Meriwether Lewis and William Clark set off on a two-year trip across the United States by foot and boat, exploring and mapping as they go.

6. Americans Robert Peary and Matthew Henson and four Inuits are the first people to reach the North Pole in 1909.

7. Norwegian Roald Amundsen was first to the South Pole in 1911, and first to traverse the Northwest Passage between the Atlantic and the Pacific.

8. In 1960, Jacques Piccard and Don Walsh reach the ocean's deepest point, 10,911 m (35,797 ft) down.

9. In 1961, Soviet cosmonaut Yuri Gagarin is the first person to travel into space. He flies all the way around the world.

Sir Francis Drake's ship, the *Golden Hind*.

Michael Asher and Mariantonietta Peru were the first to cross the Sahara desert, on foot and by camel, in 1987. Hot!

Ed Stafford, in 2010, was the first person to walk the length of the Amazon River. Steamy!

Barbara Hillary was the first African American woman to ski to both Poles in 2011.

Hillary was also part of the team that crossed Antarctica via the South Pole in 1958!

Edmund Hillary and Tenzing Norgay were the first people to climb Everest.

A pirate is a person who robs a ship at sea.

Quit squawking.

PIRATES AHOY!

Centuries ago, the only way to journey long distances was to travel by boat. But watch out – pirates sailed the seas, hoping to steal treasure and even ships!

GOLDEN AGE

Piracy has been around as long as ships have sailed. But during the Age of Exploration, pirates were everywhere, as ships loaded with treasure crossed the oceans. The era from 1650 to the 1730s became known as the Golden Age of Piracy.

THE JOLLY ROGER

How do you know a pirate ship may attack? The crew hoist a Jolly Roger flag. A popular flag was black with a skull and crossbones.

PIRATES HALL OF FAME

Meet some of the best-known (and most terrifying) pirates ever to sail the seas.

FRANCIS DRAKE (c. 1540–1596)

Captured a haul of Spanish spices, gold, silver and other valuable treasures in the Americas

BARTOLOMEU PORTUGUÊS (1600s)

Helped write the list of rules known in pirate lore as the Pirate Code

ROCK THE BRAZILIAN (c.1630–c.1671)

Pesky Dutch pirate who robbed treasure ships off the coast of Port Royal, Jamaica

FRANÇOIS L'OLONNAIS (c. 1635–c.1668)

French pirate who plundered Spanish treasure ships sailing in the Caribbean

BLACKBEARD (c. 1680–1718)

In charge of four ships and a crew of 200 pirates, with a thick black beard and fearsome appearance

ANNE BONNY (c. 1700–c.1782)

One of the few fearless female pirates at sea, this Irish American woman joined a pirate crew as a teenager

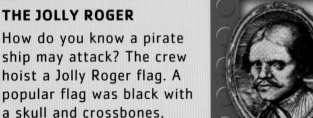
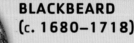

5 pirate things to say

1. THAR SHE BLOWS (THERE'S A WHALE USING ITS BLOWHOLE) 2. SHIPSHAPE (TIDY)
3. SCUTTLE (TO SINK YOUR OWN SHIP)
4. SCALLYWAG (A RASCAL)
5. HORNSWOGGLE (TO CHEAT)

GRUB'S UP

On a long voyage, food was scarce and a bit gross. Meat was often rotten and bread filled with tiny bugs called weevils.

Check your biscuits for weevils!

LIFE ON A PIRATE SHIP

Old sea dogs had to put up with a lot on a ship. They could spend months at a time at sea. Conditions were cramped, there was no way to get exercise and the food options were limited.

Crow's nest

Foremast

Topsail

You're under arrest, pirate! Now hand over that, erm, EMPTY treasure chest . . . Oh, rats.

Mainsail

Bowsprit sail

Don't mess with me, I've got a short fuse. So do my cannons.

Do you like my peg-leg pose?

Bowsprit

Mainmast

Anchor

COMPLETE WITH HIDDEN TREASURE.

AHOY! FIVE FIERCE JOBS ON A PIRATE SHIP

Listen up, me hearties! Life on a pirate ship wasn't all about sailing and stealing. There was plenty of work to do, too. From the captain down to the cabin boy, everyone on board had a job to help keep things shipshape.

SAILING MASTER

The sailing master was reponsible for the navigation of the ship. There weren't many good maps around, so plotting a ship's course took a lot of guessing. If pirates captured a ship with an expert sailing master aboard, they often forced him to join their crew.

BOATSWAIN

The boatswain was in charge of the sails and rigging and swabbing (cleaning) the deck. He was also an expert at making complicated knots from rope.

CAPTAIN

You might imagine a pirate captain was all-powerful on the ship, but in most cases that was not true. The pirates voted for a captain they looked up to. He was only fully in charge during a battle. At other times, the crew could replace him.

QUARTERMASTER

The captain's right-hand man was the quartermaster. He ran daily life, keeping everyone in line and sorting out any squabbles. He also organized the food and accounts on the ship.

The "powder monkey's" job was to run the gunpowder from below deck to the cannons during a battle.

GUNNER

Boom! The gunner was in charge of firing the cannon. It was hardly a blast. Cannons were hot and smoky, and accidents were common. It took six pirates to aim, fire and reload while the gunner gave the orders.

We've got the treasure! If we'd lost it, the crew would definitely have voted us off the top spot.

Where's the quartermaster? He's in charge of sorting out all the booty.

49

THE WILD WEST!

Criminy! The Wild West wasn't called "wild" for nothing! It was full of varmints – dangerous animals and notorious bandits. Throughout the 1800s, settlers moved to the western edge of the United States. They went to start new lives but what they ALSO found was rip-roaring adventure.

I'm rounding up the bandit and I need your help.

WANTED

COWPOKES

With all the wide, open spaces in the West, there was plenty of room for raising cattle. Cowboys were in charge of rounding up the huge herds.

ROLLIN', ROLLIN', ROLLIN'

Many people came to the West on wagon trains – groups of covered wagons. They travelled for miles across trails, stopping only to sleep and eat.

DOWN AT THE FORT

To keep safe, western settlers built hundreds of forts. These protected homes and kept traders' goods safe.

FULL STEAM AHEAD!

In 1869, the Transcontinental Railroad made it faster and cheaper for people and goods to get to the West.

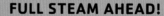

BUILD IT! **HEY, COWPOKE! BUILD YOUR OWN WILD WEST TOWN AND KEEP**

BOOM TOWNS

Little towns sprung up all over the West. Settlers built trading posts, hotels, banks, mills and jails, connected by wooden boardwalks.

In the Wild West the lawmen were just as legendary as the outlaws. But they'll never catch me ...

WANTED

ONE BAD-MANNERED BANDIT

Wanted for crimes of horse-stealing and train-robbing.

★ REWARD OF $5,000.00 ★
MOST WANTED IN THE WEST

CALIFORNIA GOLD RUSH

People came from all over the world to try their luck at "prospecting" – looking for gold. The population of California grew so fast it was made a US state in 1850. When the gold ran out, many left, leaving ghost towns and tumbleweeds behind.

In 1848, a carpenter discovered gold nuggets in California. The rush was ON!

Gold nuggets

WHAT IN TARNATION!

If you want to get by in these parts, you'd better learn to speak the local lingo, cowpoke.

▶ **Howdy** Hello

▶ **Giddy up!** Get going!

▶ **Dude**
Someone not from the West

▶ **Ain't worth a hill o' beans**
Worthless

▶ **Yellow belly** Coward

▶ **Vamoose** Leave quickly

▶ **Doggie** A cow

IT SAFE WITH A FANTASTIC FORT.

Polar explorers made many scientific discoveries. They were also great poets and painters.

POLAR HEROES

Norwegian Roald Amundsen and Englishman Robert Scott raced to reach the South Pole in freezing Antarctica in 1911. Scott sailing on his ship the *Terra Nova* (pictured). Amundsen reached the Pole on December 14, 1911. Scott arrived there on January 17, 1912. Stories of extreme hardship and heroism from the Antarctic journeys circulated around the world. They have inspired explorers ever since. People push themselves to their limits — and beyond — to find out more about our world.

Collect rocks? Well, collect some rocky info on page 56.

Better keep my eye on that volcano on page 60. It's about to blow.

High there! Get the lowdown on mountains on page 64.

EARTH IS

The LEGO® minifigures have whizzed with us through history. Now it's time for a tour of our planet. Earth is a ball of rock, dotted with towering mountains, punctured by fiery volcanoes,

There's water, water everywhere on page 66.

It's snow joke, the weird weather facts on page 70 are abominable.

Blustering bagpipes! The weather is wild and windy on page 72.

AWESOME

shaken by earthquakes, carved by rivers and battered by raging storms. And it still looks beautiful! Let's meet Earth, the ultimate force of nature.

Earth rocks. Yeah!

ROCKS AND MINERALS

Forming on or under the Earth's surface, rocks are hard, solid materials made from minerals. Our Earth is a rock-making machine. Rocks are created, then heated, squished or worn away into new rocks. At the centre of the Earth, rocks melt and the whole process starts again.

ROCKS

All rocks belong to three groups based on how they form: sedimentary (in layers), igneous (volcanic), or metamorphic (changed by heat and pressure).

Pink granite

Peridotite

Conglomera

Flint

Pumice

Migmatite

Limeston

MINERALS

Most rocks are made from natural ingredients called minerals. Minerals form into solid shapes called crystals. There are more than 5,000 different kinds of mineral.

Dioptase

Iron

Copper

Silver

GEMS

Some minerals are very rare, or have beautiful colours. These can be cut and polished into sparkling gems and made into jewellery. The rarest gems are extremely valuable.

The Earth's core is made from molten rock (it is hot enough there to melt rock). I'd better not hit rock bottom!

Sapphire

Malachite

Tiger eye

Ruby

Topaz

Lapis laz

ULURU

Rising from the desert plain in the centre of Australia, Uluru is the largest monolith (a really mega-big rock) in the world. It is 3.6 km (2.2 miles) long. It extends several miles deep into the ground. No one knows exactly how far.

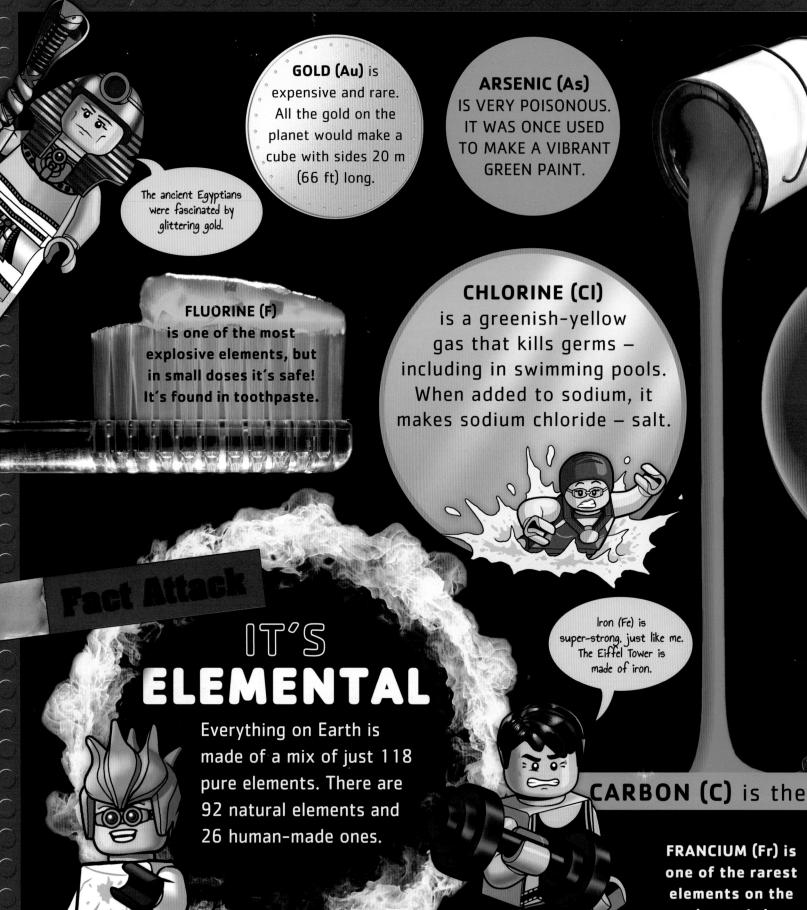

GOLD (Au) is expensive and rare. All the gold on the planet would make a cube with sides 20 m (66 ft) long.

The ancient Egyptians were fascinated by glittering gold.

ARSENIC (As) IS VERY POISONOUS. IT WAS ONCE USED TO MAKE A VIBRANT GREEN PAINT.

FLUORINE (F) is one of the most explosive elements, but in small doses it's safe! It's found in toothpaste.

CHLORINE (Cl) is a greenish-yellow gas that kills germs — including in swimming pools. When added to sodium, it makes sodium chloride — salt.

Iron (Fe) is super-strong, just like me. The Eiffel Tower is made of iron.

Fact Attack

IT'S ELEMENTAL

Everything on Earth is made of a mix of just 118 pure elements. There are 92 natural elements and 26 human-made ones.

CARBON (C) is the

FRANCIUM (Fr) is one of the rarest elements on the planet. It is believed that less than 28 g (1 oz) exists on Earth.

Time for a glass of milk!

CALCIUM (Ca)
We have 1 kg (2.2 lbs) of calcium in our bodies. It is essential for bones to grow. It is also used for making cement.

HYDROGEN (H)
BY MASS 75% OF THE VISIBLE UNIVERSE IS HYDROGEN.

Stars shine because they are changing hydrogen into helium.

HELIUM (He)
Helium is so light that it can escape Earth's gravity. That's why balloons filled with helium float up.

SULPHUR (S)
IS A YELLOW, ODOURLESS ROCK. BUT WHEN MIXED WITH HYDROGEN IT SMELLS OF ROTTEN EGGS.

OXYGEN (O)
MAKES UP ABOUT 21% OF EARTH'S ATMOSPHERE.

Ooooo, I can float, too.

CURIUM (Cm)
IS SO RADIOACTIVE, IT GLOWS IN THE DARK.

NEON (Ne)
is a gas that glows when electricity passes through it.

most vital element of life. Humans are about 20% carbon.

GALLIUM (Ga)
is a metal that melts in your hand. Scientists trick colleagues by making forks out of it!

PLATINUM (Pt) is the most expensive metal in the world.

Those humans are made up of 28 elements. It can't be hard to make one. 1 spoon of sodium, 1 spoon of copper . . .

59

Come to Hawaii and check out the world's largest active volcano. Mauna Loa is 120 km (75 miles) wide!

VOLCANOES

Hold on to your hard hats, Earth is blowing its top! When the pressure gets too much, volcanoes blast lava from Earth's boiling core high into the sky. The clouds of smoke and ash can be seen from space!

MOLTEN MAGMA

Earth's surface is like a jigsaw puzzle of rocky plates that float on softer, jellylike rock. When two plates collide, rock melts to form magma, a red-hot liquid rock. Sometimes, this bursts through Earth's surface. It's an eruption!

Right now, about 20 volcanoes are erupting somewhere in the world.

FIRE MOUNTAIN

Underground pools of magma build up and up until the pressure becomes too great. The magma is forced up through cracks, causing an eruption. Layers of hardened ash and lava cool around the crater, often creating a cone-shaped mountain called a stratovolcano.

ash cloud

layers of hardened ash and lava

lava

crater

main vent

magma pool, or chamber

MINI PICS

Stand aside! The volcano may blow its top!

There may be lava and smoke and ash!

 BUILD IT!

IMAGINE A SUPER-SIZED VOLCANO

BOILING RED RIVER

Above ground, magma is called lava. It can be 12 times hotter than boiling water. It pours from a volcano at speeds of up to 100 kph (60 mph), burning everything in its fiery path.

ISLAND INVENTOR

When a volcano erupts under the sea, the lava cools, hardens and piles up. Eventually, the rock rises up out of the water, creating a volcanic island, such as those of the Galapagos or Indonesia.

EXPLOSIVE FACTS

Magma can reach 1,300°C (2,400°F).

Magma can form almost 100 km (60 miles) below ground. Magma chambers are not so deep.

The word *volcano* comes from the Roman god of fire, Vulcan.

Yellowstone National Park sits on a supervolcano.

There are volcanoes under icecaps in Iceland.

A supervolcano is capable of ejecting more than 1,000 km³ (240 cubic miles) of material in an eruption.

When Mount Vesuvius erupted in 79 CE, it buried the town of Pompeii in Italy. The ash preserved some people like mummies.

You're a bit late.

This is Mount Fuji in Japan. It last erupted 300 years ago!

I'm studying the volcano with sensors so we can warn everyone if there's a problem!

Oh! OK! Let's go and put out a real fire!

NOW BUILD IT! USE RED AND ORANGE BRICKS TO MAKE LAVA FLOW.

EARTHQUAKES

Earth's crust is on the move. Little by little, huge blocks of crust called tectonic plates collide or separate, causing earthquakes, volcanoes and tsunamis. Most earthquakes are mild tremors but, very occasionally, they are strong enough to cause great damage.

FAULT LINES

Gigantic plates of rock make up the jigsaw puzzle of Earth's surface. The plates are constantly moving – about 2.5 cm (1 in) each year. The plates meet along fault lines, but they don't slide easily past each other. They push and shove, and pressure builds and builds until it has to be released, shaking the ground as an earthquake.

SEISMIC STUDIES

Some people think that birds and other animals can predict a quake!

Seismologists study earthquakes. They use seismographs to measure ground movements too tiny for humans to feel. They try to predict the time, location and magnitude of quakes.

THREE TYPES OF MOVEMENT ALONG FAULT LINES

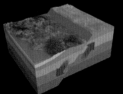 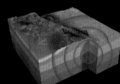 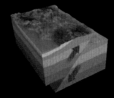

Normal fault: hanging block drops

Strike-slip fault: blocks move sideways

Reverse fault: hanging block moves up

SAN ANDREAS FAULT

This 1,300-km (800-mile) sleeping giant in California, USA, is capable of quakes above magnitude 8 on the Richter Scale.

MAP SHOWING VOLCANO AND EARTHQUAKE SITES AROUND THE WORLD

earthquakes occur along the Ring of Fire

Pacific Ocean

Fault lines frame the Pacific Ocean, and it is here that 90% of all earthquakes occur. This circle of seismic activity is nicknamed the Ring of Fire because it is home to 452 volcanoes.

Earthquakes are snow joke for mountain folk like me. They cause landslides and avalanches.

5 of the worst earthquakes ever

1. VALDIVIA, CHILE, MAY 22, 1960: MAGNITUDE 9.5 ON RICHTER SCALE, MOST POWERFUL QUAKE SINCE 1900
2. ALASKA, USA, MARCH 28, 1964: MAGNITUDE 9.2, MOST POWERFUL QUAKE IN US HISTORY
3. HONSHU, JAPAN, MARCH 11, 2011: MAGNITUDE 9.0, TRIGGERED A TSUNAMI
4. TANGSHAN, CHINA, JULY 28, 1976: MAGNITUDE 7.5, STRUCK A DENSELY POPULATED AREA
5. HAITI, JANUARY 12, 2010: MAGNITUDE 7.0

My top tip: don't make top-heavy buildings. Heavy roofs topple easily in a quake.

TOUGH TOWERS

A dizzying 634 m (2,080 ft) tall, the Skytree towers over Tokyo. Japan lies in the Ring of Fire, so this tower was specially built to resist quakes. It has a concrete shaft and oil-filled devices to absorb an earthquake's energy.

GIANT WAVES OF DESTRUCTION

Tsunami means "harbour wave" in Japanese. It is a series of huge waves caused by an earthquake under the sea. On December 26, 2004, a quake in the Indian Ocean off the coast of Sumatra, Indonesia, triggered waves 30 m (100 ft) tall and caused destruction in 14 countries.

The fault is about 16 km (10 miles) deep.

Robots can help with rescue and recovery missions after a quake.

THE RICHTER SCALE

A scale that measures the strength of an earthquake.

2

MINOR

3

2.5 or less
Usually not felt, but can be recorded by seismograph

4

LIGHT

2.5 to 5.4
Often felt, but causes only minor damage

5

MODERATE

5.5 to 6
Slight damage to buildings

6

STRONG

6.1 to 6.9
May cause major damage in populated areas

7

MAJOR

7 to 7.9
Major earthquake causing serious damage

8

GREAT

8 or more
Especially destructive near its epicentre (strongest point)

MOUNTAINS

Mountains rise all over the world from Earth's rocky crust, on land and from under the ocean. The tallest form when two of Earth's plates collide, buckling up thousands of metres, dominating the landscape.

Early Swiss goatherds communicated across valleys by yodelling. YODEL-AY-HEE-HOO!

MAKING MOUNTAINS

Most mountains are fold mountains. They form where two plates push together. Fault-block mountains form when faults or cracks in the Earth's crust force some materials up, some down, and blocks of rocks become stacked. Dome mountains form when melted rock underground pushes up. Volcanic mountains are formed after eruptions, when the lava cools.

The Sierra Nevada mountains are fault-block mountains.

Mount Fuji in Japan is a volcanic mountain.

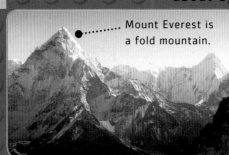
Mount Everest is a fold mountain.

THE TOP OF THE WORLD

The summit of Mount Everest, in the Himalaya mountain range in Asia, is the highest point on Earth, at about 8,850 m (29,035 ft).
New Zealander Edmund Hillary and Nepalese Tenzing Norgay were the first recorded people to reach the top, on May 29, 1953, after a climb up the southern face.

MINI PICS

Show me, oh great Yeti, how to conquer Everest.

RRRRRRRgh. I'm not a tour guide!

Take me to Everest base camp? I can climb from there.

RRRRRRRgh . . . oh, all right. Follow me.

BUILD IT!   MAKE A BASE CAMP STOCKED WITH EVERYTHING YOUR

10 things you might find inside a climber's backpack

1. HIGH-ALTITUDE STOVE   2. ICE AXE   3. RIMLESS ANTI-FOG POLARIZED GOGGLES
4. CRAMPONS   5. MOBILE PHONE AND RADIO   6. TABLET COMPUTER   7. ULTRA-LIGHT
TENT AND SLEEPING BAG   8. OXYGEN BOTTLES   9. RECOVERY DRINKS   10. IN 1953,
HILLARY AND NORGAY, THE FIRST PEOPLE TO CLIMB EVEREST, FUELLED UP ON
TINNED FISH, LEMONADE, CHICKEN-NOODLE SOUP, APRICOTS AND HOT TEA.

In 2008, Pemba Dorje climbed Mount Everest in 8 hours and 10 minutes, a world record.

MOUNTAIN WILDLIFE

▶ **Bumblebees**
In 2008, bumblebees were discovered on Mount Everest, 5,500 m (18,000 ft) above sea level! They are thought to be the highest-living insects ever.

▶ **Mountain goat**
The hooves of mountain goats have soft inner pads, like climbing shoes. The pads help them grip steep rocky surfaces.

▶ **Snow leopard**
This powerful big cat lives in the eastern Himalayas. It can leap the length of four cars in one bound, and its tail acts as a blanket.

▶ **Mountain gorilla**
High in the mountains of Central Africa, these gorillas keep warm with thick, shaggy fur.

MINUTES LATER

Everest grows 4 mm (0.16 in) a year. He'll never conquer my mountain!

Are we there Yeti?

With winds of 320 kph (200 mph) and temperatures of -62°C (-80°F), it's tough in the Himalayas. Unless you're a Yeti.

CLIMBERS NEED.

ADD A YETI'S CAVE IF YOU DARE!

RIVERS AND LAKES

Water is a force to be reckoned with. Rivers cut canyons and fill lakes, while icy glaciers bulldoze valleys. But without water, we'd be ... well, thirsty. So, let's turn on the tap and go with the flow!

Nearly half of all fish species live in lakes and rivers.

The water in an estuary is brackish – salty and fresh. Not salty enough for me! Back to sea!

An estuary is where a river meets the sea.

EARTH-MOVING RIVERS

Rivers transport water to animals and plants. They also transport the land itself, powerful enough to wear down mountains and carry them to the sea. Every year, rivers deliver about 18 billion tonnes of material to the ocean.

CARVING CANYONS

Stones tumbling in a river pummel the riverbed. Over thousands of years, the river digs deep valleys and canyons, such as Arizona's Grand Canyon in the USA, which is more than 1.6 km (1 mile) deep.

SHAPING MOUNTAINS

Glaciers are rivers of compacted ice that move slowly down mountains. Over thousands of years, they sculpt and carve the rock. They leave behind deep valleys, fjords, or rounded hollows that join together in a pointed peak, like the Matterhorn mountain in the Alps.

WATER CYCLE

Water is always being recycled, in the water cycle! Rain fills lakes and runs into rivers that empty into oceans. Rainwater also seeps underground and runs towards the sea. When water heats up at the surface, it evaporates, turning into water vapour. This rises into the sky and ...makes rain!

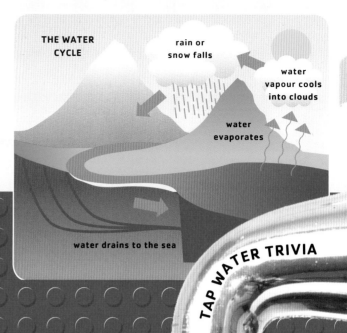

THE WATER CYCLE

rain or snow falls

water vapour cools into clouds

water evaporates

water drains to the sea

Lake Superior, clean and clear

LAKES ARE GREAT . . .

. . . especially the Great Lakes! Michigan, Huron, Erie, Ontario and Superior, are lakes on the border between Canada and the USA that together form the largest area of freshwater on the planet. They are so big, they can be seen from space.

Where do Great Lake ghosts live? Lake Eerie!

FOUR GREAT LAKE FACTS

Lake Superior really is superior. It is big enough to contain all the other Great Lakes combined.

Lake Erie and Lake Ontario are connected to the Niagara River and the Niagara Falls.

When French explorers discovered a vast inland sea, they called it *le lac supérieur*, meaning "upper lake".

Storms in the lakes can cause shipwrecks. But if you do fall in, there are 30,000 islands to swim towards. Goggles on!

TAP WATER TRIVIA

The water we drink is the same water the dinosaurs drank.

Water is cleaned and piped into homes from surface-water and underground reservoirs.

A person can live a month without food, but about one week without water. Get drinking!

Water doesn't hang around in your stomach. It leaves about five minutes after drinking, heading for the bladder.

Cold water is more dense than hot water, so it sinks. Ice floats – it is less dense than water.

A dripping tap can waste about 24 litres (5 gallons) a day. Water is precious. Be waterwise and make a splash!

Local Pemon people call the Falls Kerepakupai-Meru, which means "waterfall of the deepest place".

ANGEL FALLS

Angel Falls in Venezuela is the highest waterfall in the world, dropping 979 m (3,212 ft) off the top of Auyantepui mountain. It is 19 times higher than the famous Niagara Falls in Canada. The waterfall, which formed 130 million years ago, is one of the world's most dizzying, dazzling natural wonders.

WILD, wEiRd AND WACKY
WEATHER EVENTS

1. Snow rollers are created when a strong wind picks up a chunk of snow and rolls it into a giant ball. Ice work!

2. In 2010, Hungarians thought they were going hopping mad when a shower of frogs fell on them!

3. A severe hailstorm in Mississippi, USA, surprised locals by dropping a 20-cm (8-inch) gopher turtle!

4. In 2011, after major flooding in Ipswich, Australia, people were flabbergasted to see several sharks swimming down the road!

5. In 2010, giant hailstones as big as soccer balls – 20 cm (8 inches) in diameter – fell in South Dakota, USA.

6. Golf balls once fell from the skies in Florida, USA. They were thought to have been picked up by a tornado.

7. In 2012, California, USA, experienced record-breaking boiling-hot rain!

8. In 2013, a 9-m (30-ft) wall of ice, an "ice tsunami", crept towards homes from a lake in Minnesota. It moved 30 cm (1 ft) per second. It partially buried the houses, shattering windows and doors.

70

9. Er Wang Dong in China is a cave with a cloud! It is so large that it has its own weather system.

10. Tornado Alley, USA, sees more tornadoes each year than any other place on Earth. Once, in a single month, 758 tornadoes hit.

11. In 2015, mysterious orange snow fell in Russia. It is thought to have been coloured by the red sand of the Sahara desert.

EXTREME WEATHER

A scientist who studies weather is called a meteorologist. I'm usually called, erm, crazy.

Hurricanes, twisters and blizzards all stir up a storm on Planet Earth. Let's find out what a tornado sounds like, why snow looks white and just how hot a bolt of lightning is. Get ready for weather's wild side.

HOWLING HURRICANES

▶ A hurricane (also called a cyclone or typhoon) forms over tropical oceans

▶ Moisture in the air warms up, rises and condenses into large storm clouds.

▶ Strong winds circle upwards around the hurricane's calm central area (the eye).

▶ Most hurricanes are huge – more than 483 km (300 miles) wide.

▶ Hurricanes are given a first name from a list made at the start of the hurricane season.

TERRIBLE TORNADOES

▶ Tornadoes are funnels of air that twist down from storm clouds and travel across the land as fast as a car.

▶ With winds that can spin at 483 kph (300 mph), twisters sound like freight trains hurtling along.

▶ One thunderstorm can spawn several twisters, known as a tornado family.

▶ Tornadoes usually turn anti-clockwise in the Northern Hemisphere, but clockwise in the Southern Hemisphere.

Be careful over the United States. It has about 1,000 tornadoes every year.

The largest snowball fight had 7,681 people!

What's a tornado's favourite game? Twister.

FREEZING FACTS

▷ A snowflake is a collection of tiny ice crystals, and a hailstone is a ball of ice. Sleet is a mix of rain and snow.

▷ The largest snowflake ever was the size of a pile of dinner plates!

▷ Snow is clear, not white. As the colours in light bounce through the ice crystals, they combine to appear white.

▷ A blizzard blows snow at more than 56 kph (35 mph), while freezing rain coats everything with an icy glaze.

FRIGHTENING LIGHTNING

▷ Lightning bolts are huge electrical charges created when ice and water inside storm clouds rub together.

▷ Thunder is the noise lightning makes. We see lightning before we hear it because light travels faster than sound.

▷ A lightning bolt is five times hotter than the surface of the Sun. Sizzle!

▷ There are more than 3 million flashes of lightning worldwide every day.

▷ Look out for lightning in sandstorms, volcanic eruptions and tornadoes, too!

HOME on EARTH

"There's no place like home," and that saying goes for the millions of living things on our planet. There's life on Earth everywhere, from the bottom of the oceans to the tops of the tallest mountains. Have an animal adventure with the LEGO® minifigures.

Velociraptor means "speedy thief". RUN!

DINOSAURS

For 160 million years, these incredible creatures ruled the world. Their fossils have been found on every continent. Dinosaur means "terrible lizard", but not all of them were terrible and none were lizards! Every year new dinos are discovered.

TRIASSIC PERIOD

250 to 200 MYA (million years ago).
There is only one supercontinent, called Pangaea, on Earth. The dinosaurs appear during this period.

Herrerasaurus

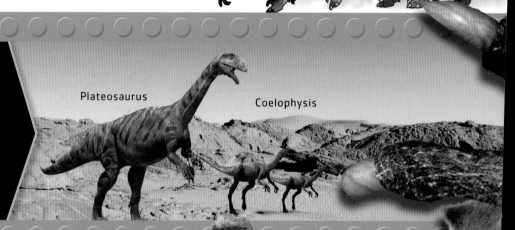

Plateosaurus

Coelophysis

JURASSIC PERIOD

199 to 145 MYA.
Pangaea starts to split apart. Dinosaurs diversify, the giant sauropods appear.

Barapasaurus

Stegosaurus

Compsognathus

Monolophosaurus

CRETACEOUS PERIOD

145 to 65 MYA.
Dinosaurs are many and varied. Giant reptiles rule the seas and flying reptiles rule the skies. 65 million years ago, the big dinos suddenly disappear.

Torosaurus

Carnotaurus

Oviraptor

Psittacosaurus

BUILD IT!   IMAGINE YOU'RE A PALEONTOLOGIST WHO HAS DISCOVERED A NEW

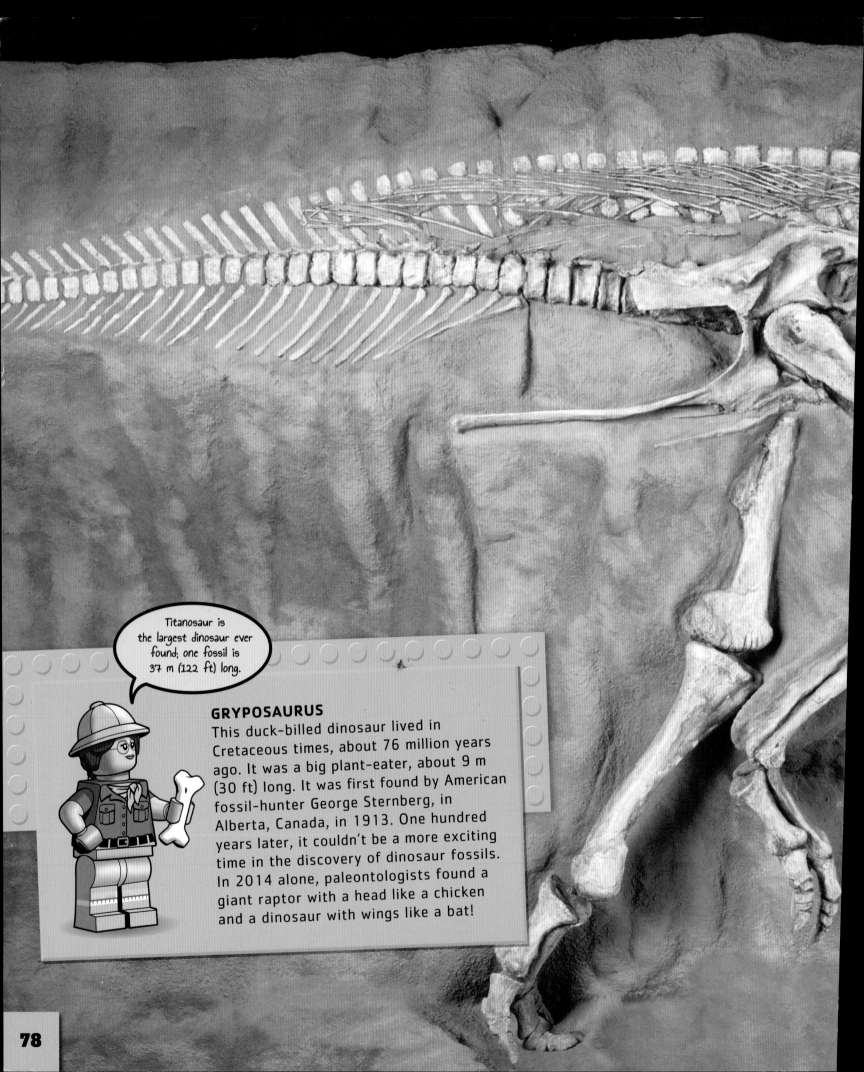

Titanosaur is the largest dinosaur ever found; one fossil is 37 m (122 ft) long.

GRYPOSAURUS

This duck-billed dinosaur lived in Cretaceous times, about 76 million years ago. It was a big plant-eater, about 9 m (30 ft) long. It was first found by American fossil-hunter George Sternberg, in Alberta, Canada, in 1913. One hundred years later, it couldn't be a more exciting time in the discovery of dinosaur fossils. In 2014 alone, paleontologists found a giant raptor with a head like a chicken and a dinosaur with wings like a bat!

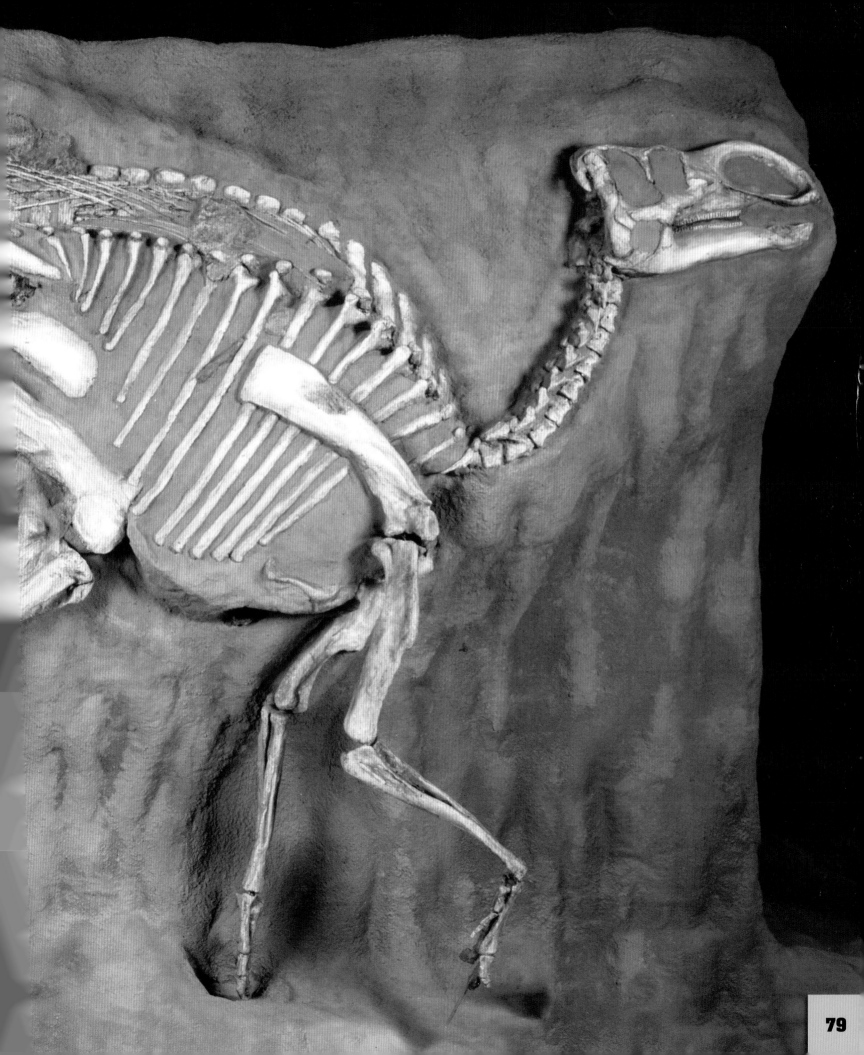

RAINFOREST

Imagine exploring a hot, damp forest with trees as tall as 20-storey buildings. All around, you hear the noise of hoots and howls, buzzes and screeches. Welcome to the tropical rainforest.

It's a jungle out there!

This place is crawling with animals, but the mighty Aztecs once made their home in the rainforests of central and southern Mexico.

WHY ARE THEY A BIG DEAL?

Rainforests produce about 25% of the oxygen that we breathe every day. The plants also absorb carbon dioxide (CO_2), cleaning the air. So take a deep breath and thank – and protect – the rainforest.

A rainforest area the size of a football field has

1,500 FLOWERING PLANT SPECIES, 750 TREE SPECIES, 125 MAMMAL SPECIES, 400 BIRD SPECIES, 100 REPTILE SPECIES, 60 AMPHIBIAN SPECIES, 150 BUTTERFLY SPECIES.

The Amazon rainforest in South America is the largest rainforest in the world.

IN THE JUNGLE

▶ **Blue morpho** butterflies are so bright that pilots flying overhead can spot them.

▶ A river won't stop an **armadillo**. It can jump in, hold its breath for six minutes and run across the bottom to the other side.

▶ The **jaguar**, a top predator, not only climbs trees but is also an expert swimmer. A jaguar attack? Cat-astrophic.

▶ The **poison dart frog** can be some of the most brilliant and beautiful colours on Earth.

▶ The **tree boa**'s babies are red, orange or yellow. Like a sandwich left behind the sofa, many turn green as they age.

▶ The male **great hornbill** hides the female and their chicks inside a tree and feeds them through a tiny hole.

▶ Twisty vines called **lianas** can grow as thick as your leg.

▶ **Leafcutter ants** chomp up and take away huge slices of leaf to feed a crowd of millions.

Keep your leaf, Mr Ant! We'll snack on chocolate, made from cacao beans from the rainforest.

RAINFORESTS PROVIDE US WITH:

Oxygen	Chewing gum
Rubber	Coconut oil
Medicines	Shampoo
Coffee	Cinnamon
Chocolate	Cocoa butter
Cashew nuts	Vanilla

Octopuses have **brain cells** in their **tentacles**. So their tentacles can think for themselves!

THE CALL OF THE **BUSH CRICKET** IS AS LOUD AS A CHAINSAW.

A tarantula can live for 2 years without food.

Some tarantulas throw barbed hairs at their enemies!

Honeybees can count to four and recognize landmarks to locate their hives.

A flamingo can only eat with its head upside down.

CRAZY BUT COOL ANIMAL FACTS

Proving why animals are endlessly interesting to find out about. Go figure!

Gorillas have unique nose prints just like humans have unique fingerprints.

Jewel beetles can sense forest fires from **80 km** (**50 miles**) away.

Some

Sloths are so slow that algae grows on their fur.

82

A tarsier's **eyes** are each the **size** and **weight** of its brain.

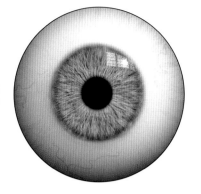

Many lizards shed their tails when threatened by an enemy. The tail carries on wiggling!

Lizards' tails usually grow back again, sometimes in different colours!

THE STAR-NOSED MOLE HAS 22 TINY TRUNKS THAT SMELL AND FEEL.

ANTEATERS EAT **30,000** ANTS A DAY.

Houseflies hum in the key of F.

The **Komodo dragon** can eat **80%** of its own body weight in one meal.

Female **lions** do almost all of the **hunting** for their family, which is called a **pride.**

chameleons' tongues are longer than their bodies.

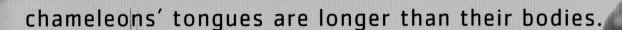

A cricket has ears on its knees.

A blue whale's heart is the size of a small car.

POLAR BEARS HAVE BLACK SKIN.

A spider's silk is one of the strongest materials on the planet.

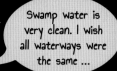

SWAMP LIFE

About 6% of the world's land surface is swampy. Swamps filter groundwater, are havens for wildlife and protect against flooding. So jump on an airboat for a swampy adventure and take a look at what lurks in the murk.

MINI PICS

WELCOME TO THE SWAMP

BUILD IT! CREATE A SWAMP, WITH AN AIRBOAT THAT CAN TAK

SWAMP RECIPE

Marshes and swamps are both soggy spots. The difference is what grows there. Trees can grow in swamps, while no woody plants grow in a marsh.

A swamp

A marsh

Ahoy there! Saltwater mangrove swamps along tropical coasts make it hard to land.

AT HOME IN A SWAMP

Alligators, frogs and fish live in the nutrient-rich waters, with animals like birds and monkeys living in the trees above. Most are harmless to humans, but not so harmless to each other ...

▶ A **mudskipper** is a fish-out-of-water. It mud-wrestles other skippers for its own patch of mud bank.

▶ A **heron** is a spear-fishing bird with lightning reflexes.

▶ The **crocodile** is king of the swamp. These prehistoric creatures are usually docile, unless they are hungry ...

▶ A **snapping turtle** has a red tongue tip that looks like a worm. It lures curious fish towards its gaping jaws.

▶ The **green anaconda** is a giant snake that can reach 8.8 m (29 ft) long. Wild pigs, deer and even jaguars better look out for this slick swimmer.

Swamps are excellent animal homes. There's plenty of water and lots to eat. And you'll love the neighbours.

What's that splash?

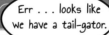

Err . . . looks like we have a tail-gator.

Yikes! See you later, alligator.

Airboats are powered by an air propeller and skim over shallow water. They can't reverse but they can go at 96 kph (60 mph).

LIFE AT THE POLES
SUPER HOT, SUPER COLD FACTS

1. Penguins live in the Antarctic, around the South Pole. Polar bears only live in the Arctic, around the North Pole.

2. More than 90% of all the ice on the Earth's surface is at the Poles.

3. If all the ice in Antarctica melted, the global sea levels would rise around 61 m (200 ft).

4. Antarctica is the driest, windiest, emptiest, coldest place on Earth.

5. The Inuit of the Arctic have a kiss called "kunik". Greeters rub noses and sniff cheeks and hair.

6. The town of Churchill, Canada, in the Arctic has a jail for naughty polar bears.

7. Arctic reindeer have eyes that are golden in the summer and blue in the winter.

8. A species of Arctic frog freezes when it gets too cold. Its blood stops flowing until it thaws in warmer weather.

9. Emperor penguins are 1.2 m (4 ft) tall. Fossilized penguins show that penguins once stood 1.5 m (5 ft) tall!

10. The average thickness of the Antarctic ice is about 1.6 km (1 mile). Now that's ice!

11. Including its islands and floating ice, Antarctica is about one-and-a-half times the area of the United States.

12. In 1978, Argentinian Emilio Palma became the first child born on Antarctica.

RULERS OF THE ICE

The largest land carnivores in the world roam the Arctic sea-ice. Polar bears have fur thicker than any other bear, which even covers their feet. The bears are magnificent swimmers. A layer of blubber keeps them warm as they push through the water with front feet like oars. They don't stop. Polar bears have been tracked swimming 100 km (60 miles) without a break.

FIVE FEMALE EXPLORERS OF EARTH'S WILDEST PLACES

These five amazing women share a thirst for adventure. They have visited the farthest reaches of our planet – and beyond! Travelling by foot, kayak, submersible or even spacecraft, these amazing explorers have taught us much about Earth's wild places.

THE SUB-MARINER

Sylvia Earle is an American marine biologist. She has swum with humpback whales, discovered many new species, and even lived in an underwater lab. Having designed and piloted deep-sea submarines, Sylvia now works to protect ocean habitats.

THE CONSERVATIONIST

Austrian Ida Pfeiffer (1797–1858) made two round-the-world trips collecting many important plant and animal specimens. She explored on her own at a time when this was unusual for women. Pfeiffer wrote two best-selling books about her experiences.

AWESOME ADVENTURER

Helen Thayer, born in New Zealand in 1937, has walked across the Sahara and Gobi deserts, kayaked the Amazon River, climbed mountains, and even lived with wolves for six months. In 1988, she trekked to the North Pole with a dog called Charlie.

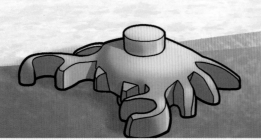

THE MOUNTAIN CLIMBER

Japanese climber Junko Tabei has climbed 69 mountain summits. In 1975, she became the first woman to reach the top of Mount Everest. She made a dangerous crawl across an icy ridge to reach her goal.

THE SPACE EXPLORER

American astronaut Mae Jemison soared to great heights on the space shuttle *Endeavour* in 1992. She was a Mission Specialist, performing several scientific experiments while in space. Mae orbited Earth 127 times during her 190-hour spaceflight!

In 1979, Sylvia Earle dived to a record 381 m (1,250 ft) wearing a special diving suit.

Junko Tabei was also the first woman to climb the Seven Summits – on seven continents.

DESERT LIFE

Be they burning sand or icy plateaus, deserts are definitely dry. Meet the hardy animals and plants that live there.

WHAT MAKES A DESERT?

To qualify as a desert, land must receive less than 25 cm (10 inches) of rain each year. And that's it! Deserts cover a third of Earth's land.

DESERT BLOOM!

Cactus plants are spiky water stores. Other desert plants have extra long roots to tap into water deep underground. Among the grains of sand, dormant seeds happily blow in the wind . . . until it rains. Then BLOOM! The desert is transformed.

DESERT RECORDS

Antarctica is the coldest desert. At the South Pole, the highest temperature ever recorded was a chilly −12.3°C (9.9°F). The Gobi desert is classified as hot. But in winter, it can be −40°C (−40°F), making it the coldest hot desert. The Sahara is one of the hottest deserts, with temperatures that can fry an egg – over 47°C (116.6°F).

Desert plants like jojoba make lush face creams. We ancient Egyptians have been using them for years. And look how beautiful we are . . .

 BUILD IT!

BUILD A DUNE

The Marathon des Sables is a 251-km (154-mile) running race across the Sahara desert.

WELCOME SIGHT

Oases, pools of water in the desert, form from underground water sources. Sand easily blows into water, so people often plant a protective ring of palms around oases.

AMAZING ANIMALS

Animals have developed ingenious ways to survive.

▶ The **thorny devil** is a lizard of the Australian Outback. Tiny channels between its thorny scales lead water to its mouth.

▶ The **sidewinder snake** moves in such a way that only two points of its body are in contact with the hot sand at a time.

▶ The **camel** is the "ship of the desert". It has long lashes and closeable nostrils to keep out sandstorms. Its wide feet act like snowshoes.

▶ The **African pixie frog** buries itself underground in a mucus membrane. It can stay like that for several years, until new rain wakes it up.

I dig your shades, meerkats. Those black eyes prevent the Sun from reflecting back into your eyes.

CAVE LIFE

Slide down ropes into the deep, dank world of caves. Some animals visit; others spend their entire lives in the dark.

It's DEEP, man!

I'm off spelunking. Wanna come?

CAVE CREATURES

▶ The **olm salamander** swims in cave pools, blind, pale, with super senses, including the ability to sense electricity.

▶ **Crickets** have long legs and antennae to guide them through the dark. They're found in old mines as well as caves.

▶ Bracken Cave in Texas, USA, has the largest **colony of bats** in the world. It's estimated that 20 million bats hang out there in the summer.

▶ When winter arrives, **North American black bears** hibernate in dens, made in caves or other sheltered places. They've eaten so much in the summer, they can live off stored body fat.

▶ Though usually pretty small, **giant cave spiders** can have legs more than 30 cm (12 inches) long.

Watch out for vampire bats! They feed on blood!

4 totally cavernous caves

1. IN THE **CAVE OF CRYSTALS,** MEXICO, THE CRYSTALS ARE BIGGER THAN A HOUSE. 2. THE **GLOWWORM CAVE IN** NEW ZEALAND IS FULL OF THOUSANDS OF WORMS THAT GLOW LIKE STARS. 3. SAY GOODBYE TO DAYLIGHT WHEN YOU ENTER THE **KRUBERA CAVE, GEORGIA**. IT'S THE DEEPEST IN THE WORLD AND STRETCHES OVER 2 KM (1.2 MILES) TOWARDS THE EARTH'S CORE. 4. THE **SON DOONG CAVE** IN VIETNAM IS THE LARGEST KNOWN CAVE IN THE WORLD. IT IS FILLED WITH COUNTLESS WONDERS, INCLUDING STALAGMITES THAT ARE 70 M (230 FT) TALL.

Caves make good shelters from the hot Sun as well as the icy rain and snow.

Not all early people lived in caves, though, especially if bears got there first.

Speleology is the name for the science of caves.

Potholing, caving or spelunking is the name for exploring caves for fun.

A stalactite hangs from the roof of a cave. It forms slowly, drip by drip, as dissolved minerals are deposited in tiny specks by the drips.

A stalagmite forms when dissolved minerals from drips build up on a cave floor.

The ocean is full of strange creatures. Starfish have no brains and no blood.

OCEAN LIFE

Earth's five salty oceans – the Pacific, Atlantic, Indian, Southern and Arctic – cover more than 70% of its surface. The weather on top and the currents beneath move water between oceans. One drop of water, in time, could travel around the world.

CORAL REEF

Coral is a living organism of polyps that grows in the ocean's sunlit zone. Coral attacks its food with stinging cells and gets its colour from the algae that live inside it. Coral reefs are the most diverse ocean habitat, providing food and homes for many sea creatures.

Giant brain coral

Jellyfish

Flying fish

Sunlit zone: 0–200 m (0–650 ft). Heat and light are in abundance. Colourful fish and coral reefs are found here. Plants live in this zone only.

Crab

Twilight zone: 200–1,006 m (650–3,300 ft). The light is dim in this zone. Many fish are silver-coloured.

Squid

Sea spider

Cookiecutter shark

Dark zone: 1,006–3,962 m (3,300–13,000 ft). Say goodbye to sunlight. It's pitch dark. Many fish produce their own light.

Let's go to the dark zone. I want to find a dragonfish. It has teeth on its tongue!

Brittle star

FISH TALK

Fish don't have vocal cords but they can "talk". Some vibrate their muscles, some rattle their bones and some gnash their teeth to communicate. They pop, hoot, croak and bark.

8 record-breaking residents of the sea

1. FASTEST: THE SAILFISH AT 109 KPH (68 MPH) 2. BIGGEST: THE BLUE WHALE, 30 M (100 FT) LONG 3. MOST POISONOUS: THE BOX JELLYFISH 4. LARGEST PREDATORY FISH: THE GREAT WHITE SHARK 5. LONGEST BONY FISH: THE OARFISH CAN GROW TO 15 M (50 FT) LONG 6. BIGGEST CRAB: JAPANESE SPIDER CRAB, 3.7 M (12 FT) LONG 7. MOST NUMEROUS CREATURE: COPEPODS 8. MOST NUMEROUS FISH: THE BRISTLEMOUTH (A DEEP-SEA FISH)

Dolphin

Shark

Turtle

Tuna fish

Octopus

Sperm whale

Catshark

Krill

Sea star

Anglerfish

Viperfish

Watch where you swim. Some of the most poisonous creatures in the world live in the sea.

Abyssal zone: 3,962–6,096 m (13,000–20,000 ft). The water is just above freezing. Not much can survive because of the immense water pressure.

Tripod fish

Sea cucumber

Deep-sea snail

DEEP-SEA LIFE

It's pitch dark and the pressure is immense. The water is only just above freezing, and the only food is fragments sinking from above. What would live in the deep dark part of the ocean?

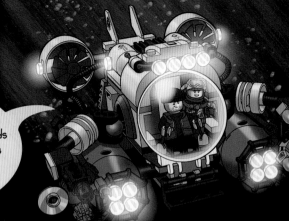

In February 2016, we heard the first ever sounds recorded from the depths of the Mariana Trench. It's a noisy place!

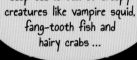

Watch out, the deep sea is full of creepy creatures like vampire squid, fang-tooth fish and hairy crabs ...

MARIANA TRENCH
The deepest part of Earth's oceans is in the Mariana Trench, in the Pacific Ocean. It is almost 11 km (7 miles) deep. Only three people have ever been down to the bottom.

EXPLORING THE DEPTHS

Some parts of the ocean are as deep as Everest is high. Despite this, scientists have developed marine robots and high-tech submersibles that can explore the dark depths.

A 7.6-cm-thick (3-in-thick) titanium pressure hull keeps it from imploding.

The *Shinkai 6500* is a Japanese submersible that can dive to 6,400 m (21,000 ft).

SHINKAI 6500

Two pilots and one researcher can operate within it.

Hey! It's a shipwreck! I'll look for some lost treasure.

Huh? There's a light in there. Someone's got there first!

Arggh! It's a lantern shark that glows in the dark! I'm out of here!

MINI PICS

BUILD IT! **MAKE A DEEP-SEA SUBMERSIBLE READY TO EXPLORE THE OCEAN DEPTH**

BIOLUMINESCENCE

At 1,800 m (6,000 ft) below the surface
is a circus of extraordinary deep-sea
creatures. Many produce light in their bodies,
called bioluminescence, which they use for
communication, finding food and defence.
The anglerfish has a bioluminescent
lure to attract prey.

Scientists have
explored only 1% of
the ocean depths.

SHARK BITES
TO SINK YOUR TEETH INTO

1. Sharks are super smellers. A shark can sniff out a colony of seals up to 3 km (2 miles) away.

2. A shark loses about one tooth a week, but there are more behind it, waiting to pop into place. Some sharks use up over 10,000 teeth in a lifetime.

3. Prehistoric shark Megalodon was a 18-m (60-ft) giant with teeth that were 18 cm (7 in) long.

4. Almost 50 different kinds of shark have photophores – organs that give off light.

5. Statistically, bee stings are more dangerous to humans than shark bites.

6. Sharks don't really like the taste of people. They may bite them out of curiosity before spitting them out and finding something more delicious.

7. Although most sharks are grey or brown, some are pink, yellow or blue.

8. After a big meal, a great white shark can go for two weeks or so without feeding again.

9. Sharks don't have bones. Instead, their skeletons are made of lightweight and flexible cartilage.

10. A great white shark gives birth to two to ten babies, called pups. Pups can swim right after they are born.

INVENTION

Imagine creating or thinking up something totally new. Something no one has ever built or thought of before. Your invention might be as simple as

There is an amazing new wave on page 108.

See some top tech on page 110.

Read about the rise of the robots on page 112.

AND DISCOVERY

a toothbrush with a built-in dispenser, or something that changes the lives of millions of people. First, though, you will need some inspiration. Let the minifigures introduce you to some of the greatest creators, discoveries and inventions in history.

FIVE SUPER SCIENTISTS AND THE BEST IDEAS EVER!

Geek alert! Meet five of the greatest scientists of all time. They had big brains and even bigger ideas about how to explain some of the trickiest stuff in the universe, from gravity to space and time.

GALILEO GALILEI
(1564–1642)
Italian brainiac Galileo Galilei built his own telescope without ever seeing one. He explored the night sky, discovering the four largest moons of Jupiter, mountains and valleys on the surface of our moon, sunspots and the movements of Venus.

ARCHIMEDES
(c. 290–212 BCE)
This ancient Greek genius explained how machines work, from levers and pulleys to a screw to raise water. He worked out pi (the ratio of the circumference of a circle to its diameter) to 99.9% accuracy.

ISAAC NEWTON
(1643–1727)
Inspired by watching an apple fall from a tree, Isaac Newton explained that gravity is everywhere. He was famous for his three laws of motion, showing how forces cause an object to move. He also developed the branch of maths known as calculus.

MARIE CURIE
(1867–1934)
Polish chemist Marie Curie discovered two new chemical elements: polonium and radium. These elements helped medical scientists develop X-ray machines and fight cancer. In 1911, Curie became the first person to win two Nobel Prizes, the top award for scientists and other thinkers.

$$E = mc^2$$

ALBERT EINSTIEN
(1879–1955)
German-born physicist Albert Einstein's Theory of Relativity explained many mysteries of the universe and showed how space and time are linked. Einstein wrote a famous equation: $E = mc^2$. E is an object's energy, m its mass, and c is the speed of light.

Science is amazing! All the knowledge we get from testing out our ideas can help us to explain everything in the universe.

Maybe that explains why you have a particularly large head.

10 HELPFUL
INVENTIONS

1. Fireworks were invented more than 2,000 years ago when a cook in China was experimenting with kitchen ingredients.

2. The oldest documented artificial human body part is a toe made of wood and leather. It was found attached to an ancient Egyptian mummy.

3. Restaurant-owner George Crum invented crisps in 1853. His customers kept saying that the fried potatoes weren't thin enough...

4. Make it rain! In 2014, scientists worked out a way to fire rain-making laser beams into clouds. The beams may also cause lightning.

5. In 1931, Goventosa de Udine built a motorized monowheel – a motorbike with one huge wheel encircling the driver. It could travel at up to 150 kph (93 mph).

6. Three students in England invented a motorized bath in the 1960s. It had three wheels, a number plate and a rubber-duck horn.

7. Get off my lunch! An anti-theft lunch bag appeared in 2008. Mould printed on the bag made the sandwich inside look...mouldy!

8. An invisibility cloak was revealed in 2011. It used a mineral that bends light rays, tricking the eyes to create an illusion of invisibility.

9. In 2013, a five-year-old invented an all-in-one toothbrush, with a toothpaste dispenser built in. Just squeeze. No mess and no lid!

10. James Stuart Blackton invented animated movies! His 1906 short animation *Humorous Phases of Funny Faces* was the first to be made using a standard film format.

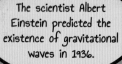

The scientist Albert Einstein predicted the existence of gravitational waves in 1936.

GRAVITATIONAL WAVES

Sometimes there are discoveries made in science that change the way we think about the universe. In 2016, scientists detected gravitational waves for the first time. These were ripples in the universe made when two black holes collided and sent out waves so powerful they squeezed and stretched space and time. Now we have a new way to explore the universe.

INVENTION TIME LINE

When there is a tricky problem that needs solving, people invent things. Whether it's a way of working, a product or a machine, inventions help us to do all kinds of things. Job done!

Cave people invented using natural stuff like stone, wood and rocks.

EARLY INVENTIONS

Many inventions don't just appear, they change through history. Sometimes inventions are made by turning existing ideas into even better ones.

c. 1,000,000 BCE Cave people invented ways to make fire.

c. 3500 BCE The invention of the wheel got people going.

2000 BCE The Babylonians invented the number zero.

140 BCE Paper was invented in China.

WHAT'S NEXT?

A good idea doesn't always lead to a great invention. A new gadget has to be in demand, easy to make and protected from copying.

1826 The first photograph (of roofs and chimneys) was taken by Joseph Niépce of France.

1829 The first train, Stephenson's *Rocket*, sped along at a record-smashing 48 kph (30 mph).

1876 The box telephone was invented by Alexander Graham Bell. His first words were to his assistant: "Mr Watson, come here."

1878 Thomas Swan invented the glass light bulb and Thomas Edison invented a long-lasting filament.

Ralph H. Baer is my hero. He invented video gaming in 1967 with the first console.

TECH TIMES

Breakthroughs in technology lead to a burst of inventions. Smaller and cheaper gadgets appear. The power of a roomful of the first computers can fit inside a mobile phone.

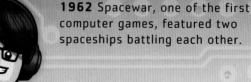

1962 Spacewar, one of the first computer games, featured two spaceships battling each other.

1965 The first touchscreen device was a tablet made by British engineer E. A. Johnson. It was used by air-traffic controllers until 1995.

Speech bubble: People are inventing robots with artificial intelligence.

Speech bubble: Soon, robots may be smarter than people!

MEGA INVENTIONS

Some inventions are so important that they lead to countless other inventions. The wheel, for example, is used in everything from cars and aeroplanes to computer hard drives.

Speech bubble: We launched the Hubble Telescope into space in 1990.

1088 Shen Kuo, a Chinese scientist (1031–1095) discovered that the Earth acts like a huge magnet. He invented the magnetic compass.

1455 Invention of the moveable-type printing press.

1608 The telescope helped people look closer at the celestial bodies in the sky.

1783 The French Montgolfier brothers launched the first hot-air balloon capable of carrying people. The balloon flew over Paris for 25 minutes.

Speech bubble: In 1895, German Wilhelm Röntgen made a winning invention: X-rays. He won the first Nobel Prize in physics.

1885 The first car, a three-wheeler with no roof that chugged along at 13 kph (8 mph) was built by German Karl Benz.

1895 The Lumière brothers patented the cinematograph. Modern cinemas were born.

1903 The *Wright Flyer*, the first aeroplane, made its maiden voyage, rising 37 m (120 ft) and flying for 12 seconds.

1926 The televison was invented by John Logie Baird of Scotland. In 1953, the first colour TV show aired in the USA, and in 1988 flatscreen televisions first appeared.

1973 Motorola produced the first handheld mobile phone. It worked for 30 minutes and took 10 hours to recharge.

1977 The Apple 2, a user-friendly personal computer, was invented by Stephen Wozniak and Steve Jobs.

1983 A number of tech innovations lead to the development of the modern Internet. Tim Berners-Lee invented the World Wide Web.

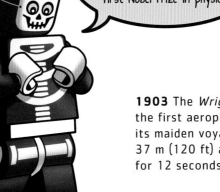

2000 Bill Gates launched Microsoft's touch-input tablet computer. Apple popularized tablets in 2010 with the launch of the iPad.

2004 Mark Zuckerberg created a website to allow friends to connect, which became Facebook.

2005 Video-sharing website YouTube launched to allow users to upload, view, comment on and rate video content.

ROBOTS

They're here now. In the future, they'll be everywhere: an army of robots in our homes, at our schools, even inside our bodies. Bots are getting busier and brainier. The latest robots are even thinking for themselves.

I'm not here to replace you ... I'm just here for the par-tay. 24/7!

JOBS FOR THE ROBOTS

Need someone to answer the phone in ten different languages? Or switch on the TV and pass you the remote? ASIMO is the ultimate home-helper. Someday, robots may take over all our jobs, but for now we can work side by side. Thanks, buddy!

I stay safe while the bot does all the dangerous stuff.

BOT, DO YOU COPY?

FLYING SKY HIGH

One day, our skies will be filled with busy bots. Flying robots can already:

Look for underwater mines
Inspect tall bridges and buildings
Check weather from high up in the sky
Herd sheep from a hillside to their home
Wear robot bee disguises to pollinate plants
Find evidence of lost, buried ancient cities
Film big sporting events from the air
Carry medicines to disaster areas
Deliver post – and even pizza!

Someday, our bodies may be crawling with tiny nanobots, keeping us fit and healthy from the inside. Creepy!

BUILD IT!

DESIGN YOUR OWN ROBOT TO EXPLORE THE

10 things real robots can really do

1. CLEAN WINDOWS 2. WRITE COOKBOOKS 3. PLAY CARDS
4. PRACTISE TABLE TENNIS 5. BE LIFEGUARDS 6. DRIVE CARS
AND TRUCKS 7. PLAY THE PIANO 8. DELIVER ROOM
SERVICE 9. COMPETE ON TV GAME SHOWS 10. ZIP UP
ZIPS . . . AND ALL WITHOUT A BATHROOM BREAK!

To keep all those bots from crashing into planes, a new air-traffic-control system will be built.

A car-sized roving robot named *Curiosity* makes tracks across Mars, finding out about the planet's history.

Humanoid teacher-bot NAO can ask questions and understand answers. NAO is able to help people with autism to learn.

The Atlas robot is being developed to walk over rough ground, drill through rocks and climb using arms and legs, to help rescue people.

OCEANS, FLY THROUGH SPACE, OR EVEN HELP CLEAN YOUR ROOM!

MINI PICS

In the future, robots will power and move themselves — they'll just keep going!

Power-assisted suits will gve you superhuman strength!

You'll be able to *roll* up your **TABLET** like a mat.

Artificial intelligence will make computers that you can talk to just like humans.

TEMPERATURE-CONTROLLED MUGS WILL MAKE SURE YOUR HOT CHOCOLATE IS NOT *TOO* HOT.

We robots will become workers and even your friends!

SMART FRIDGES will have screens for looking up recipes. You'll also be able to see inside your fridge using your phone!

2.5-M (98-IN) TELEVISIONS WITH A PICTURE **SO SHARP** THAT NO PIXELS ARE VISIBLE **AT ALL**.

Fact Attack

A HIGH-TECH FUTURE

The future's coming and it's going to be techtastic. So sit back and switch on!

Watch movies with my eyes closed? Seeing is believing!

SOLAR-POWERED PLANES could bring clean energy to air transport.

Send an avatar to school

ACTIVE CONTACT LENSES WILL BECOME MINICOMPUTERS THAT LET YOU WATCH MOVIES AND READ MESSAGES.

Now I'll never put a foot wrong!

Look forward to trainers with self-tightening laces, made with foot-scanning technology.

DRIVERLESS CARS WILL COME TO PICK YOU UP, WITH THE PRESS OF A BUTTON ON YOUR PHONE.

DRIVE
START
STOP

CLOTHES WILL DO EVERYTHING A SMARTPHONE DOES NOW.

SPACE TOURISM WILL LIFT OFF. CHECK IN FOR A FIVE-NIGHT STAY IN AN ORBITING HOTEL SUITE.

Space begins 80 km (50 miles) above Earth.

Forget going to the shops to buy a new toothbrush. You'll be able to print one on a 3-D printer! Phones, jewellery and even food may be printed for us one day.

VIDEO GAMING GOES AR (AUGMENTED REALITY) – NO DEVICE, AND PLAYING A GAME FEELS LIKE YOU'RE IN THE GAMING REALM.

A SCANDINAVIAN COMPANY IS WORKING ON A WAY **TO TRANSLATE WHAT A DOG IS THINKING.**

OH, NO! I'll be out of a job!

Visit Venice from your sofa.

HOVERBOARDS that *really* hover, animated pets and toys that talk back are all being developed.

Zero-carbon, **sustainable cities**, like Masdar near Abu Dhabi, are under construction now.

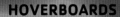

GET READY FOR **CRASH-PROOF CARS** USING RADAR, SONAR AND DRIVER-ALERT SYSTEMS.

Even I, an Alien Villainess, did not know all the facts on page 120. My fact-zapper must be broken. Hand yours over.

Yes, boss.

We are marching to Mars. Meet you there, on page 124.

3,2,1,

Is space the place you'd love to explore? Zoom into an outer-space adventure with the LEGO® minifigures! There's a

BLAST OFF!

whole galaxy of facts to uncover. Visit the planets and meet the men, women and machines exploring the universe. Turn the page and let's lift off!

MOON LANDING

There is no air, weather, or life of any kind on the Moon – so why go? Because getting there and surviving on its surface was the greatest human challenge of all time. Let's join moonwalkers Neil Armstrong and Buzz Aldrin on that historic first trip.

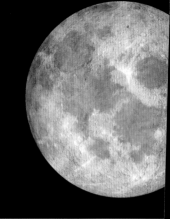

When is the Moon not hungry? When it's full.

TRIP TO THE MOON

In 1969, three US astronauts left Earth on a mission called Apollo 11. They were launched by *Saturn V*, a powerful rocket. When the Apollo 11 crew reached the Moon, a lunar landing module named *Eagle* dropped down to the surface. Astronauts Neil Armstrong and Buzz Aldrin were the first people to set foot on the Moon. They collected soil samples and left a flag.

Armstrong said that setting foot on the Moon was "one small step for [a] man, one giant leap for mankind".

Apollo 11 launching

Did you know that only 12 people have ever walked on the Moon?

And none since 1972! I wasn't even a mini minifigure then.

Someday robots will run a space lab on the Moon. Look, there it is!

MINI PICS

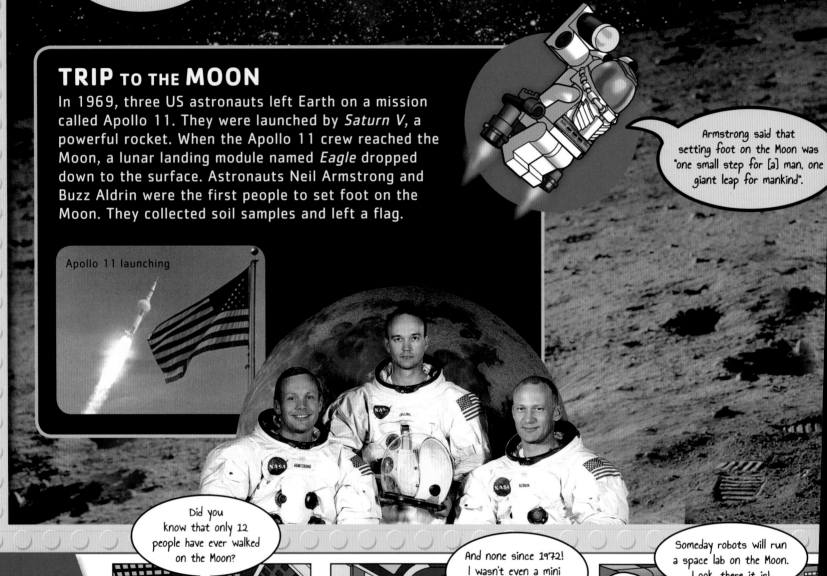

10 things left on the Moon by astronauts of past missions

1. BAGS OF PEE 2. EMPTY PACKETS OF SPACE FOOD 3. BLANKETS 4. A HAMMER
5. A PAIR OF BOOTS 6. BACKPACKS 7. USED WET WIPES 8. FOOTPRINTS 9. A RAKE
10. TWO GOLF BALLS (HIT IN 1971 BY APOLLO 14'S ALAN SHEPARD WITH A CLUB HE
HAD SMUGGLED INTO SPACE)

A VIEW TO REMEMBER

The crew members of Apollo 8 were the first to see an "Earthrise", when they flew around the Moon in 1968.

Aldrin and Armstrong explored the Moon's surface for more than two hours.

Three spacesuits were designed for each astronaut – one for training, one for flight and one for space.

The astronauts collected soil samples and planted an American flag.

With no wind or weather to disturb them, these footprints will remain for millions of years.

IT'S MOON-TASTIC!

The Moon is not round – it's egg-shaped.

The Moon has no atmosphere, so the sky appears black.

Humans may walk on the Moon again. There have been plans to build a base there, to use as a stepping stone to reach Mars.

The Moon doesn't shine. It reflects light from the Sun.

During the day, the temperature on the Moon can reach 123°C (253°F). At night, it can drop to a chilly −233°C (−387°F).

It takes three days to fly to the Moon from Earth.

Houston, we have contact!

Hey, what are you doing? Where are you going?

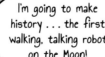

I'm going to make history . . . the first walking, talking robot on the Moon!

Later, space dudes.

Earth travels around the Sun at **108,000** kph (67,000 mph). Hold on tight!

1 MILLION Earths could fit inside our Sun.

THERE ARE **TWO** GOLF BALLS ON THE MOON.

MORE THAN **95%** OF THE UNIVERSE IS INVISIBLE TO US.

THERE ARE ABOUT THREE SEPTILLION STARS. THAT'S **3,000,000,000,000, 000,000,000,000.** GIVE OR TAKE ONE OR TWO.

If you stood on Mercury, the Sun would look **2-and-a-half** times bigger than it does on Earth.

Fact Attack

OUT-THERE NUMBERS IN SPACE

Astronaut means "star sailor" ... cool!

Volcanoes on Mars are **100** times bigger than those on Earth.

Attention, humans! Prepare your squishy brains to absorb some mind-boggling facts. Read on!

The black hole

A single asteroid can contain more gold than has ever been mined on Earth. Mine, all mine!

There are about **half a million** pieces of space junk orbiting Earth. Heads up!

It would take 800 years to fly a jet plane to Pluto.

We are **149,500,000** km (92,900,000 miles) from the Sun. But don't forget to wear sunscreen.

THE SUN ACCOUNTS FOR **99.8%** OF THE MASS OF OUR SOLAR SYSTEM.

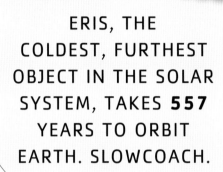

ERIS, THE COLDEST, FURTHEST OBJECT IN THE SOLAR SYSTEM, TAKES **557** YEARS TO ORBIT EARTH. SLOWCOACH.

THERE ARE **SIX** AMERICAN FLAGS ON THE MOON.

A full NASA space-suit costs **$12 million**.

JUPITER HAS **67** MOONS.

IT WOULD TAKE **130** DAYS TO DRIVE A CAR TO THE MOON.

A single day on Mercury equals **176** days on Earth. Now that *is* upside down.

closest to Earth is about **10,000** light-years away.

THE AVERAGE DISTANCE BETWEEN STARS IS **32 TRILLION** KM (20 TRILLION MILES).

The Moon is moving about **3.8** cm (1.5 in) away from our planet every year. See you later!

The **smallest stars found are 19 km (12 miles) wide**.

SPACE STATION

The International Space Station (ISS) is a science lab orbiting Earth, about 354 km (220 miles) above our planet. It completes an orbit every 90 minutes. Look up, you might just see it!

Want to know what it's like to build the ISS? Try building one with LEGO® bricks - but put gloves on first!

Astronauts have to be sick in a "barf bag" or the chunks will float away. Yuck!

THE ISS PIECE BY PIECE

The ISS is about the size of a soccer field. For more than 15 years, separate pieces have been blasted up inside rockets to be fixed on by astronauts. Imagine trying to build while floating in a spacesuit! One astronaut dropped her tool bag in November 2008. It's been orbiting Earth ever since.

SUIT FOR SPACE

When the ISS needs an outside repair, it's time for a spacewalk. A spacesuit has everything an astronaut needs: oxygen, carbon dioxide removal and pressure controls. Fourteen layers protect the astronaut from scorching-hot sunshine or freezing shade. The longest space walk was 8 hours and 56 minutes.

LIVING IN SPACE

Astronauts regularly stay on the ISS for about six months. Samantha Cristoforetti stayed for 199 days at one time, the longest stay of a female astronaut, leaving in June 2015.

6 weird things to get used to on the ISS

1. NO SHOWERS – SPONGE BATHS ONLY 2. FOOD AND DRINKS STORED IN POUCHES (TO STOP THEM FROM FLOATING AWAY) 3. NO SALT OR PEPPER – THE SPRINKLES FLOAT INTO THE INSTRUMENTS, CAUSING DAMAGE 4. A TOILET LIKE A VACUUM CLEANER 5. NO BED – JUST A SLEEPING BAG FASTENED TO A WALL 6. TWO-HOUR DAILY EXERCISE SESSIONS TO STOP YOUR MUSCLES TURNING TO JELLY

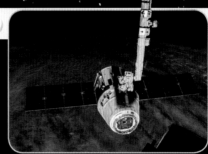

packet of space food

ESSENTIAL DELIVERIES

About four times a year, food and equipment are delivered to the ISS by unmanned spacecraft. After they've taken away waste, some of these spacecraft burn up in Earth's atmosphere.

THINGS TO DO ON THE ISS

Play football, upside down!

Chase balls of juice around the pod and catch them with your mouth.

Cry the biggest tear! Tears do not float away on the ISS – they collect in a huge water bubble on your face.

Spot countries on Earth from the viewing pod.

Go for a (space) walk – although it takes 8 to 12 hours to prepare for one!

MINI PICS

Yawn! I need a good night's sleep. Ready, Teddy?

Sleeping's a little different up here, with no up or down. Climb into your crew cabin. You don't want to float around and bump into things, so attach your sleeping bag to the wall.

Teddy, I'm attaching YOU to me. Big squeeze!

THE RED PLANET

It's super stormy, super dusty, and there's very little oxygen. But don't worry about all that! Plans are afoot to land the first humans on Mars. Are you tough enough to take a trip to the red planet? Better read this quick guide first.

It would take 271 years and 221 days to get to Mars by car. Mars is far out, dude!

WHERE IS MARS?

Mars is the fourth planet from our Sun, at a distance of 228.1 km (141.71 million miles). Its atmosphere is too thin to keep in heat. So Mars is freezing cold, with an average temperature of about −63°C (−82°F).

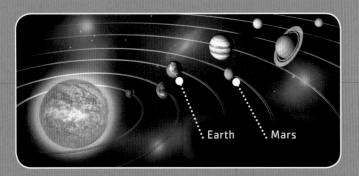

Earth · Mars

WATER ON MARS

In September 2015, new findings from NASA's Mars Reconnaisance Orbiter revealed the strongest evidence yet that liquid water may sometimes flow on Mars. Researchers saw minerals in mysterious streaks. The streaks seem to move over time as though they flow, when temperatures are above −23°C (−10°F). These flows may be related to liquid water.

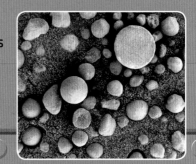

MINI PICS

Streaks of water on Mars? Send me to explore!

Hold on a sec. You might have germs from Earth.

I was just curious.

BUILD IT!

BUILD A ROVER TO SNOOP AROUND A PLANET. MAKE SURE IT CAN

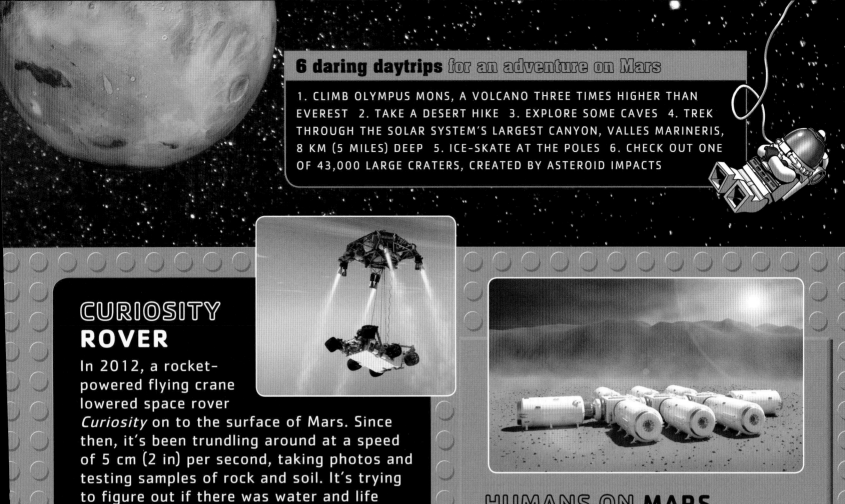

1. CLIMB OLYMPUS MONS, A VOLCANO THREE TIMES HIGHER THAN EVEREST 2. TAKE A DESERT HIKE 3. EXPLORE SOME CAVES 4. TREK THROUGH THE SOLAR SYSTEM'S LARGEST CANYON, VALLES MARINERIS, 8 KM (5 MILES) DEEP 5. ICE-SKATE AT THE POLES 6. CHECK OUT ONE OF 43,000 LARGE CRATERS, CREATED BY ASTEROID IMPACTS

CURIOSITY ROVER

In 2012, a rocket-powered flying crane lowered space rover *Curiosity* on to the surface of Mars. Since then, it's been trundling around at a speed of 5 cm (2 in) per second, taking photos and testing samples of rock and soil. It's trying to figure out if there was water and life billions of years ago.

HUMANS ON MARS

NASA is hoping to send the first astronauts to Mars in the 2030s. When they arrive, they will build a shelter to protect themselves from the cold and the solar radiation. The astronauts will also have to construct a power source to produce oxygen for breathing and growing food.

Why do those crazy Earthlings want to go to Mars? It's way too chilly!

CLIMB OVER ROCKS AND UP VOLCANOES!

EXOPLANETS

YOU WOULD NO WAY WANT TO LIVE ON . . .

1. Too easy to get lost on – Kepler-10c is 2.3 times bigger than Earth.

2. Too bad for the hair – GJ1214b is very hot and wet. Even the air is mostly water.

3. Too speedy – COROT-Exo-7b whizzes around its sun in just 20 hours. And it's scorching hot.

4. Too chilly – OGLE-2005-BLG-390Lb is the coldest planet ever discovered. Its surface temperature is about –223°C (–370°F).

5. Too fiery – Kepler-70b is a scorcher because it's super close to its sun. Its surface temperature is a sizzling 6,870°C (12,398°F).

6. Too deadly – COROT-7b rains rocks down on to oceans of lava. Ouch! There's nowhere to hide!

7. Too freaky – TrES-2b is close to its sun, but mega-dark. It's so dark, it reflects less light than coal or matte black paint.

8. Too confusing – Fomalhaut B zigzags its way around its sun, sometimes 7.2 billion km (4.5 billion miles) from it, sometimes 43.5 billion km (27 billion miles).

9. Too bling – 55 Cancri e is thought to be made completely of diamonds. And it's eight times bigger than Earth!

Let's hit the waves with some awesome boats on page 140.

You can dive deep in a submarine, too!

We're taking over planet Earth! You might want to call for an emergency vehicle on page 132.

COOL VEHICLES

Hop on board and zoom across land, sea and air. Check out the emergency vehicles that save lives, meet mighty machines building big and chase record-breaking vehicles with a need for speed. Let's go!

BIG MACHINES

Say hello to the mightiest machines on the planet as they cut, lift, push, crush and dig to build and demolish our towns and cities.

MONSTER MACHINES

Want to build big? You'll need BIG machines! Check out these monsters.

DUMPER-TRUCK GIANT

These beasts may be more than 6 m (20 ft) high and 15 m (50 ft) long. Each tyre is almost twice as tall as a person. There are driverless versions, too!

BORING BRUTE

This monster is better known as the "mole". It grips tunnel walls, then thrusts its huge cutting wheel forwards to devour solid rock.

SEA MONSTER

This is not a ship – it's the largest floating crane in the world. *Thialf* is more than 201 m (660 ft) long and has two giant cranes.

SHOVELLING BEAST

Giant diggers, more than three storeys high, can shift 8,000 tonnes of soil in one hour. These excavators cost more than £7 million each.

TERRAIN TORMENTOR

Mining excavators are the largest vehicles on Earth. They can be 213 m (700 ft) long with a 21-m (70-ft) bucket-wheel that carves into the ground.

Some crawler cranes can lift 2,700 tonnes, the weight of 600 elephants!

BUILD IT!   MAKE A TOWERING CRANE. USE STRING TO TIE ON A

INCREDIBLE CRANE

A crawler crane moves easily over bumpy ground on caterpillar tracks, and rotates to swing its long boom into place. A hook on a steel cable attaches to the load. The crane doesn't topple due to heavy counterweights on its base.

WRECKING BALL OR A LIFTING HOOK.

EMERGENCY!

Help! Call 999! Emergency vehicles whizz trained officers and equipment to the scene. These machines, adapted to save lives, are some of the most interesting vehicles of all.

Let's go! I'll bring officers and equipment. You speed on ahead!

Roger that. My top speed is 210 kph (130 mph).

FIRE-FIGHTING TRUCK
Engines have hoses, water and foam tanks, ladders, cutting tools, medical kits – and a crew of firefighters.

Breat[h] equipment me from and g[as]

TOUGH TRUCK
A steel, armour-plated police truck with fold-out shields can handle the toughest of emergencies. With four-wheel drive and large rugged wheels, bumpy terrain poses no problem for this mean machine.

TWO-WHEELED WONDER
Nimble in traffic, police motorcycles are perfect for cities. They are fitted with radios, sirens, warning lights and medical kits. This makes the bikes very heavy, so police drivers are specially trained.

DO NOT CROSS

 BUILD IT! | MAKE A RESCUE VEHICLE THAT CAN GO ON LAND AND WATER!

7 things US police officers might say

1. BOLO: BE ON LOOKOUT (PRONOUNCED "BO-LOW") 2. HOUSE MOUSE: AN OFFICER WHO RARELY LEAVES THE POLICE STATION 3. CIVVIES: NON-UNIFORM CLOTHING WORN FOR UNDERCOVER WORK 4. BACK-UP: EXTRA HELP 5. COPY: UNDERSTOOD 6. FRISK: SEARCH SOMEONE 7. STAKE OUT: WATCH AN AREA SECRETLY

Check out my yellow floats, or pontoons. They help me land on the sea!

Some fireboats can pump water 122 m (400 ft) into the air.

Don't squirt me! I'm trying to land!

FIREBOAT
In just one minute, some fireboats can suck up 189,271 L (50,000 gallons) of water and pump it at a fire on a ship or in a port.

AIR AMBULANCE
In remote places, special planes transport patients to faraway hospitals. Each year, the 66 planes of Australia's Flying Doctor Service fly the distance of 30 return trips to the Moon to help 100,000 people.

HOVERING HELICOPTER
Police helicopters have searchlights and heat sensors to track criminals by night. Helicopters can take off and land in small awkward places. One even landed on the summit of Mount Everest in 2005!

I'm the Fire Chief. I don't ride in the truck – I have a car that acts as a mobile command unit.

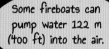

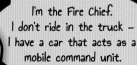

IN THE AIR

Right now, almost one million people are cruising through the skies in planes coordinated by air-traffic control. But look up – you might also see a hot-air balloon, a drone or an ultralight.

The highest skydive began 42 km (26 miles) above the Earth!

Good afternoon, this is your pilot speaking. We are cruising at an altitude of 9,144 m (33,000 ft).

Did the pilot just say we're cruising with attitude?

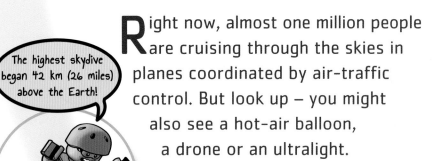

FAST AND HIGH

July 28, 1976, was a busy day for the Lockheed SR-71. One "Blackbird" flew to a record height of 25,929 m (85,069 ft). Another hurtled along at 3,530 kph (2,193 mph), a speed record that still stands today.

London's Heathrow Airport processes 53 million bags each year and has 48 km (30 miles) of conveyor belts.

BUILD IT!

Altitude! It means height above sea level. Cruising is the level part of the flight between ascent and descent.

Check out my supersonic jet! Jets that break the speed of sound are used to train astronauts.

My retractable skis help me land in icy Arctic lands.

With a wingspan of about 80 m (260 ft), the double-decker, four-engined Airbus 380 is the largest passenger plane of all time.

Like a go-cart with wings, a motorized ultralight can weigh as little as 113 kg (250 lbs) – less than two people.

Need a bird's-eye view to assess a forest fire or search a remote desert? Send in a drone, an unpiloted computer-controlled aircraft.

The longest runway in the world is in China. It stretches for 5.5 km (3.4 miles). The shortest, on Caribbean island Saba, is 0.4 km (0.25 miles).

A gas burner heats the air inside a colourful, billowing "envelope". The hot air is lighter than the surrounding cooler air, so the balloon rises.

SCANNING THE SKY

In a large busy airport, one plane takes off or lands every 45 seconds. Each one is monitored and instructed by air-traffic controllers in a central tower. Radar is used to plot the position of planes.

MACHINE, WITH JET ENGINES!

Becoming a rescue swimmer in the US Coast Guard is extremely tough. Only around 900 people have ever passed the training.

SEARCH AND RESCUE

Air–sea rescues can involve coordinating helicopters, seaplanes and boats. The mission is simple: to get people out of the water before they come to any major harm. Helicopters fly in to lower winchmen or rescue swimmers into the ocean or on to the deck of a stranded vessel. This team is practising a rescue with a training dummy. Helicopters and their crews are also especially helpful in mountain rescues.

FIVE RECORD-BREAKING SPEED CHAMPIONS!

Helmets on, fasten your seat belts! We're off on a hair-raising ride with some of the greatest speed champs of all time. In specially built vehicles powered by rockets, jets or simply leg muscles, these daring drivers zoomed to new world records.

ROCKET-PLANE PILOT

Faster even than the jet-engined *Blackbird* (see page 134) is the rocket-powered *North American X-15*. It has held the world speed record for a rocket-plane since 1967, when Major William J. Knight flew at 7,274 kph (4,520 mph). The *X-15* soared so close to the edge of space that its pilots were given astronaut badges.

SUPERSONIC DRIVER

In 1997, in Black Rock Desert, Nevada, USA, British driver Andy Green's car *Thrust SSC* became the first car to break the speed of sound. It hit 1,228 kph (763 mph), the fastest speed ever achieved by a land vehicle.

MOTORBIKE MASTER

The fastest person on two wheels is US motorcycle rider Rocky Robinson. In 2010, his streamlined *Ack Attack* bike zoomed to an incredible 634 kph (394 mph).

WATER WHIZ

Australian Ken Warby holds the world water-speed record. He built a "hydroplane" (water plane) in his own backyard, using wood, fibreglass and a cheap jet-engine. In 1978, his boat *Spirit of Australia* powered across a lake, reaching 511 kph (318 mph).

PEDAL POWERHOUSE

Barbara Buatois from France might say that using an engine is cheating. In 2010, she pedalled her streamlined recumbent bicycle to a cracking 122 kph (76 mph) – the fastest speed ever in a vehicle powered by a woman.

In a Formula 1 race, about 20 open-wheeled, single-seat cars zoom around the track. It's too dangerous to attempt speed records.

The Italian circuit at Monza is the fastest track.

ON THE OCEAN

Today, there are boats adapted to every need – huge supertankers piled high with containers, fishing vessels loaded with nets, inflatables for police crews, submarines for underwater adventures and powerboats built purely for speed.

Slow down, speedy!

But I'm on a powerboat! I can hit 322 kph (200 mph)!

SUPERTANKER

Steel ocean giants, more than 396 m (1,300 ft) long and 60 m (197 ft) wide, transport huge containers of goods all over the world.

FISHING VESSEL

Over 90 million tonnes of fish are caught each year. Fishing boats have powerful winches to lift the heavy nets.

POWERFUL POWERBOAT

Powerboats are long and thin. This streamlining helps them cut through the water quickly. Cockpits are reinforced with roll bars to prevent them collapsing if the boats flip.

About 3 million shipwrecks lie on the ocean floor. Perfect for treasure-hunting! Oo-arr!

BUILD IT!

MAKE A CRUISE SHIP LIKE A FLOATING CITY.

It's not race day! Stop!

He's too fast, boss! He has a pointy, streamlined boat. We're wide and round – for stability, not speed.

Me, I'm built for strength. My super-strong steel hull can carve up Arctic ice.

WATER PATROL
Police use inflatable boats – they are light and easy to transport. Gas-filled tubes keep them afloat if they take on too much water.

ANCHORS AWEIGH!
The world's largest anchor belonged to supertanker *Seawise Giant*. It weighed a colossal 33 tonnes and was 7 m (23 ft) long.

ARCTIC ICEBREAKER
With strong, shaped hulls and underwater air jets, icebreakers can cut through thick ice, moving forwards or backwards.

STEEL SUBMARINE
Every submarine has its own "crush depth", which can be up to 732 m (2,400 ft). If the sub dives to its crush depth, the water pressure will squash it like a tin can.

IT NEEDS CABINS, RESTAURANTS, SHOPS AND A SWIMMING POOL!

THE LONGEST AND HEAVIEST AEROPLANE IS THE AN-225 *MRIYA*. THIS CARGO PLANE IS 84 M (275 FT) LONG AND WEIGHS 285 TONNES.

THE FASTEST ROAD CAR YOU CAN BUY IS THE **HENNESSEY VENOM GT**. IT TRAVELS AT 435 KPH (270 MPH).

In 2002, Steve Fossett took just over 14 days to **fly non-stop around the world** in a hot-air balloon.

The longest train ever had 682 wagons, 8 locomotives and was 7.3 km (4.5 miles) long!

The FASTEST SPEED on an unaltered **lawnmower** is 98 kph (61 mph)!

Woo-hoo, life in the fast lane!

Fact Attack

The biggest privately owned superyacht is 222 m (728 ft) long. It cost more than one billion US dollars to build!

THINGS *THAT GO!*

Check out the fastest, biggest, longest trains, planes, probes, cars and even lawnmowers!

There are an estimated

KEVIN FAST pulled a 57,243-kg (26,265-pound) fire truck 30 m (100 ft) to break the world record.

Kevin has also pulled a house and a plane. Strong!

The most expensive car in the world is the **Lamborghini Veneno Roadster**. It costs £31 million.

There are at least 5,000 commercial aeroplanes flying over the United States at any one time.

THE FASTEST-MOVING VEHICLES EVER WERE THE HELIOS SPACE PROBES THAT REACHED 252,000 KPH (157,000 MPH) AS THEY RACED AROUND THE SUN.

The LEGO Group is the world's biggest tyre manufacturer. It makes **318 million tiny tyres** every year!

The largest LEGO® wheel is 10.7 cm (4.2 inches) high and belongs to the Power Puller car.

It would take 500 days to cycle to the Moon – if you pedalled at 32 kph (20 mph) without a break.

MORE THAN **21.5 MILLION VW BEETLES** HAVE BEEN SOLD. IT'S ONE OF THE BEST-SELLING CARS OF ALL TIME.

TO SHOW THEIR SIZE AND SHAPE IN THE DARK, SOME LARGE TRUCKS ARE COVERED IN MORE THAN 100 LIGHTS.

1 billion bikes in the world – double the number of cars.

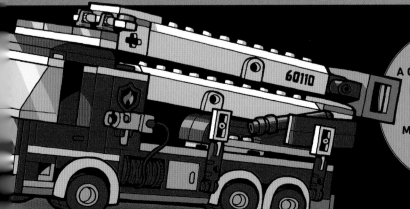

60110

A CALIFORNIAN TOWN IS FAMED FOR ITS COLLECTION OF MORE THAN 80,000 HUBCAPS!

THE LONGEST ROAD SUITABLE FOR CARS IS THE **PAN-AMERICAN HIGHWAY**. IT BEGINS IN ALASKA AND ENDS IN ARGENTINA.

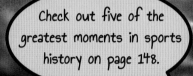

Check out five of the greatest moments in sports history on page 148.

When I see snow, I say, Go! Get with the winter sports on page 150.

Surf's up on page 152. Phew, what a wave!

SPORTS CRAZY

Are you a football fanatic, a surfer dude, a record-breaking champion, or a mighty Olympian? Or just an all-around good sport? The LEGO® minifigures are here to get sporty. They race, they leap, they throw, they score! The crowd goes crazy!

THE OLYMPICS

From gymnastics to wrestling, swimming to wheelchair tennis, there's an Olympic sport for everyone. So join in the fun at the biggest sporting event on the planet. There are medals and glory to be won.

> One ancient wrestler trained by carrying a calf every day. As the calf grew, he got stronger.

ANCIENT OLYMPICS

The first Olympics were held in 776 BCE in Greece. The games took place for four days in the city of Olympia.

Olympic Stadium, Beijing, China

FASTER, HIGHER, STRONGER (CITIUS, ALTIUS, FORTIUS)

This is the motto of the modern Olympic Games, which began in 1894. The Olympic games has been held every four years since (it has only been cancelled three times). The Paralympics began in England in 1948 and is always held in the weeks following the Olympics.

> In 490 BCE, Pheidippides, a Greek soldier, ran 42 km (26 miles) to pass a message from Marathon to Athens. The first marathon!

> USA has won a men's wheelchair basketball gold medal a record SEVEN times!

> The first female Olympic tennis champion was Charlotte Cooper in 1900. She played in a full, ankle-length dress!

14 Olympic events that really did exist . . .

1. POODLE CLIPPING 2. PLUNGING 3. SWIMMING OBSTACLE RACE
4. CROQUET 5. TUG-OF-WAR 6. SOLO SYNCHRONIZED SWIMMING
7. ROLLER HOCKEY 8. EQUESTRIAN LONG JUMP 9. ROPE CLIMBING
10. TANDEM BICYCLE 2,000-METRE SPRINT 11. ONE-HANDED
WEIGHTLIFTING 12. UNDERWATER SWIMMING 13. STANDING
HIGH JUMP 14. POLO

BUILD IT!

BUILD AN OLYMPIC TRACK FOR YOUR CHAMPION ATHLETES.

FIVE GREAT
SPORTING
MOMENTS

It's the moment sporting fans sometimes wait all their lives to see. The rare moment, when an individual or a whole team perform a sporting act so awesome that it goes down in history.

1982 NATIONAL FOOTBALL LEAGUE, "THE CATCH"

The Dallas Cowboys have dominated the NFL since 1970. There are 51 seconds of an NFC Championship game left, when Dwight Clark, of the San Francisco 49ers, makes a spectacular catch that sets up an extra kick point that leads them to a 28–27 victory. It is the end of the Cowboys' rule.

1972 CANADA V. SOVIET UNION

An eight-game showdown between the two superpowers of ice hockey. The Soviets are in the lead after the first five games. Then in a spectacular turnaround, Canada go on to win the last three games in Moscow. A last-minute goal by Paul Henderson gives the Canadians a 6–5 victory in the final game. Canada wins the series.

1986 WORLD CUP QUARTER FINAL "GOAL OF THE CENTURY"

Argentinian Diego Maradona deftly dribbles the ball past five England players and finally shoots it past the goalkeeper to score. England are devastated. Argentina wins 2–1, and goes on to win the World Cup.

2001 US OPEN, SISTERS MEET

It's the final of the 2001 US Open, between two sisters, Venus and Serena Williams. The game lasts 69 minutes. At one point, Venus smashes a 175-kph (109-mph) serve that knocks the racket from Serena's hand. Venus wins 6–2, 6–4 in a bittersweet victory.

2004 RED SOX COMEBACK

Picture this: the Boston Red Sox trail the New York Yankees three games to none in the American League Championship Series. Then, in an unprecedented success, they win the next four games to knock out the Yankees, their big rivals. The Red Sox go on to win the World Series.

The longest tennis Grand Slam final? The 2012 Australian Open men's singles final. Novak Djokovic defeated Rafael Nadal after FIVE hours, FIFTY-THREE minutes.

Ha! The longest professional baseball game lasted for 33 innings, with EIGHT hours and TWENTY-FIVE minutes.

149

WINTER OLYMPICS

Brace yourselves, it's the Winter Olympics! It's all about snow, ice and some incredible speeds. The first Winter Games was held in 1924, in France. The original five sports were bobsleigh, curling, ice hockey, Nordic skiing and skating. In 2018, the Winter Olympics will be in Pyeong Chang, South Korea.

Norway has won the most medals in Winter Olympic history.

RECORD TORCH JOURNEY
The 2014 Sochi Games torch travelled on an epic trip, including the North Pole, the bottom of the world's deepest lake and even into space, to the International Space Station.

SPEEDSTERS
For those who want speed lying down, look no further than the luge. Manuel Pfister of Austria shot down a track at a top speed of 154 kph (95.7 mph)!

Ski-jumpers launch themselves from hills up to 120 m (394 ft) high. A jumper can remain in the air for 7 seconds. That's flying!

The youngest individual gold medallist was American figure-skater Tara Lipinski, aged 15, at the 1998 Games in Japan.

X 211

SNOW CHAMP

Norwegian cross-country skier Bjørn Dæhlie is the Winter Games medal champ. He has won eight golds and four silver medals in three Olympics.

Snowboarding was introduced to the Winter Olympics in 1998. Norwegian Torstein Horgmo was the first to perform a triple cork – three flicks. Awesome!

American Eddie Eagan is the only person to have won a gold medal at both the Winter and Summer Olympics! For the four-man bobsleigh team and boxing.

Ice hockey and figure skating were originally part of the Summer Olympics.

Curling was invented in Scotland. All the stones used in curling are made in Scotland or Wales. Better keep hold of my brush!

RE THE ONLY INDOOR WINTER SPORTS. BUILD AN ARENA FOR THEM.

Officially the largest wave ever surfed was 23.7 m (78 ft) by American Garrett McNamara, 2001, off the Portuguese coast.

SURF'S UP!

Ever since Polynesian Islanders, over 3,000 years ago, picked up a wooden board and "rode" the waves, the quest to find the perfect wave has persisted. Every wave is different, and surfers learn to use their skills to keep riding them. Modern surfing is not just a sport but has become an entire culture, with cool words and fashion style.

UNUSUAL SPORTS
RECORD BREAKERS

1. To make the world's largest ever vertical skydiving formation, 164 skydivers created this giant flower in the sky over Chicago in July 2015.

2. American Darren Taylor dived 10.3 m (33 ft 10 in) into a pool of water 30 cm (12 in) deep to win the world shallow-dive record.

3. Dan Magness, from the UK, kept a soccer ball up for 26 hours using just his feet, legs, shoulders and head.

4. Christopher Irmscher, from Germany, ran the 100-metre hurdles in 14.82 seconds, wearing flippers!

5. Thaneswar Guragai, from Nepal, bounced a basketball 444 times in one minute.

6. In 2013, Japan's Kenichi Ito completed the fastest 100-metre run ON ALL FOURS in 16.87 seconds.

7. In 2006, American Daniel Smith (nicknamed The Rubber Boy) passed his body through a tennis racket 3 times in one minute!

8. The fastest skateboard speed from a standing start is 129.94 kph (80.74 mph), set by Mischo Erban in 2012.

9. In 2013, Krystian Herba, from Poland, climbed all 2,754 steps of the World Financial Center in Shanghai, China on a bike! It took 1 hour, 21 minutes.

10. In Australia, in 2012, 145 waterskiers were pulled along by a single boat.

154

STUFF

ticket to a world of culture. Open your eyes to a world of entertainment, be stunned by awe-inspiring buildings and above all, enjoy!

FIVE
FAVOURITE SOUNDS OF MUSIC

Whether you like jazz or classical, disco or rap, or just jamming to a little rock, there is a sound for everyone out there. All music has roots that can be traced back hundreds or thousands of years, but every once in a while a new sound emerges and takes the world by storm.

LET'S ROCK!

Rock music developed out of "Rock and Roll" during the 1960s. Rock bands are known for their BIG sounds. British band Led Zeppelin once reached 130 decibels during a particularly loud concert! THAT'S LOUD.

ALL THAT JAZZ

Jazz was born in New Orleans about 100 years ago, but its roots can be found in the musical traditions of both Africa and Europe. The world's largest jazz festival is the Festival International de Jazz de Montréal in Quebec, Canada. 3,000 artists perform 650 concerts, which attract over 2 million jazz visitors!

POP STARS

Pop songs are short, basic tunes that repeat choruses, melodic tunes and hooks. The "Queen of Pop" is Madonna. She is the most successful female musician of all time. She has also acted in more than 20 films. She's a busy pop star!

RAP ARTISTS

Rapping has its roots in old African storytelling from centuries ago. It has rhythmic lyrics that accompany hip hop music. The first rappers to win the Best Rap Performance Grammy were DJ Jazzy Jeff & The Fresh Prince (aka Will Smith) in 1988, with "Parents Just Don't Understand".

CLASSICAL MUSIC

Most classical music is written for orchestras, which may have up to 90 instruments, led by a conductor. The largest ever orchestra consisted of a whopping 7,224 musicians, in 2013, in Australia! They played Queen's "We Will Rock You" among other pieces.

AMAZING BUILDINGS

Some buildings invite us to slow down, look around and take in the view. They say a lot about the people who built them, the story of the times they lived in and what they wanted to leave for the future. They inspire us to create our own fantastic builds.

The Egyptians were great early architects because of our awesome pyramids.

So no one is actually going to live in that beautiful building?

As well as building the Eiffel Tower, Gustav Eiffel helped to build the Statue of Liberty.

Eight Boeing 747s could sit wing to wing on the Sydney Opera House site.

Sydney Opera House, Sydney, Australia
This was built by Danish architect Jørn Utzon and opened in 1973. The roof is made from huge, interlocking shells.

Taj Mahal, Agra, India
Believed to be one of the most beautiful buildings in the world, this was built by the Mughal emperor Shah Jahan (ruled 1628–1658) to house the tomb of his wife.

Eiffel Tower, Paris, France This was built by the engineer Gustave Eiffel in 1889, who said that it celebrated science and industry. It was made up of 18,000 iron pieces.

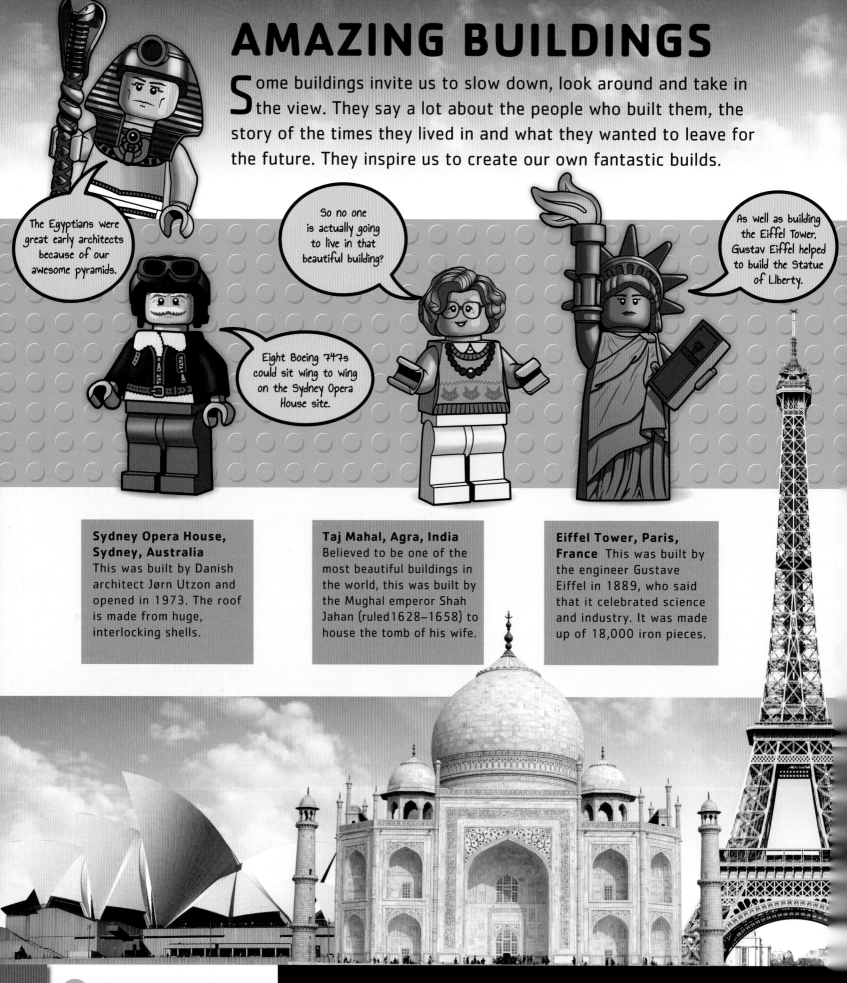

BUILD IT!   MAKE THE MOST FANTASTIC BUILDING YOU CAN IMAGINE!

4 epic LEGO® brick builds

1. THE KENNEDY SPACE CENTER, USING 750,000 LEGO BRICKS, COVERING 140 SQ M (1,506 SQ FEET) 2. A FULL-SIZE BRICK HOUSE WITH A HOT SHOWER AND A BED, USING 3.3 MILLION BRICKS 3. HOGWARTS SCHOOL OF WITCHCRAFT AND WIZARDRY, USING 400,000 BRICKS 4. ALLIANZ ARENA, A STADIUM BUILT FROM 400,000 BRICKS WITH 30,000 MINI FANS INSIDE!

Empire State Building, New York, US When this building opened on May 1, 1931, it was the tallest building in the world, standing at 381 m (1,250 feet) tall.

St Basil's Cathedral, Moscow, Russia Built in the 16th century by Russian ruler Ivan the Terrible, it has nine chapels, each with a dramatically decorated dome.

161

CRAZY CONSTRUCTIONS

1. Take a trip to Gettorf, Germany, to check out this upside-down house. All the furniture inside is topsy-turvy, too.

2. The John Hancock Tower in Boston, US, used to sway in the wind, making people feel seasick.

3. Sweden's Ice Hotel melts every summer. It is rebuilt in the winter with 10,000 tons of compacted snow.

4. Architects in Holland are developing the first house made entirely on a 3-D printer.

5. A treehouse made from an aeroplane nestles in a Costa Rican jungle as part of a luxury hotel.

6. A hotel in Shanghai has a glass-bottomed swimming pool suspended from the 24th floor. Perfect for peering down on the street below.

7. A Bulgarian house is shaped like a snail. It is five storeys high, has no straight walls or corners and is made from eco-friendly materials.

8. In Rotterdam, in the Netherlands, 38 houses that are perfect cubes are situated at different angles so they look like trees in a forest.

9. Selfridges department store in Birmingham, England, is curved, and covered in 15,000 shiny aluminium discs on a blue background.

The tallest LEGO® tower was built by 18,000 builders (many of them children) in Milan, Italy, in 2015.

AMAZING ARCHITECTURE

Want to build something incredible? Look no further than the Nagoya Science Museum in Japan. Inside the ball-shaped dome is the world's biggest planetarium, which is 35m (115 ft) in diameter. The dome is suspended between two 12-storey-high "green walls" filled with plants. The best architecture can spark the imagination of young builders like you. Get creative and make an incredible structure. What will you build today?

IN THE THEATRE

Theatre, as a form of entertainment, developed 2,500 years ago. The ancient Greeks built great amphitheatres to perform specially written funny, sad or political plays. Over the years, many forms of theatre evolved. Let the show go on!

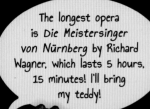

The longest opera is *Die Meistersinger von Nürnberg* by Richard Wagner, which lasts 5 hours, 15 minutes! I'll bring my teddy!

In an opera, all the words are sung. Wolfgang Amadeus Mozart (1756-1791) wrote 22 operas!

Swan Lake is considered the most popular ballet of all time. Oh, to be a swan!

Cats is one of the longest-running musicals of all time. Purrr-fect!

"Break a leg" means good luck in theatre. If I break a leg, I'll be in a cast for months!

Actors are called thespians after Thespis, the first actor.

Mozart wrote his first opera when he was only 12 years old.

Ballet began in Italy in the 16th century, and soon became popular in France.

The first modern musical, *The Black Crook*, was based on a book by Charles M. Barras. It opened in 1866.

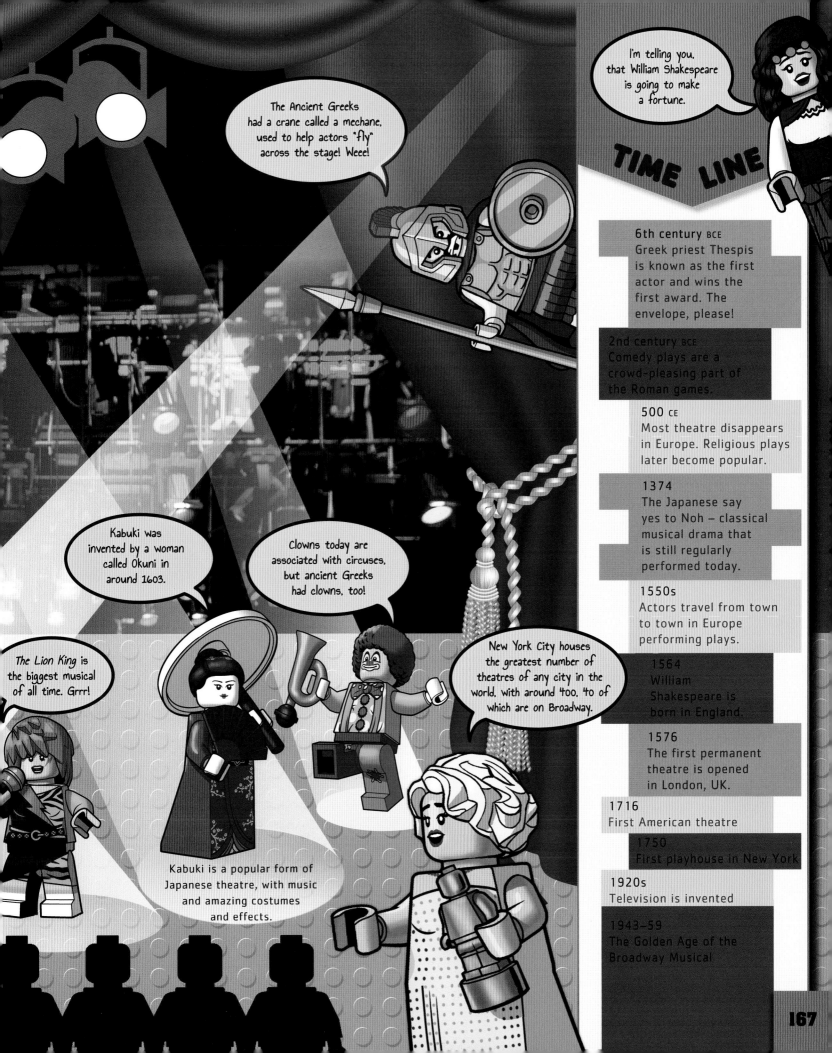

DISSES
BY WILLIAM SHAKESPEARE

1. Toads, beetles, bats, light on you!

2. Away, you mouldy rogue, away!

3. You scullion! You rampallian! You fustilarian! I'll tickle your catastrophe.

4. Truly, thou art ... like an ill-roasted egg.

5. You elf-skin, you dried neat's tongue ... you stock-fish!

6. Is his head worth a hat?

7. He's a most notable coward, an infinite and endless liar, an hourly promise breaker.

8. Pray you, stand further from me.

9. The rascally, scald, beggarly, lousy, pragging knave.

10. I do wish thou wert a dog, that I might love thee something.

11. Thou art a boil, a plague-sore, an embossed carbuncle, in my corrupted blood.

12. Away, you three-inch fool!

13. Methinks thou art a general offense.

14. Eat my leek.

Dumbledore means "bumblebee" in old English. J. K. Rowling chose the name for Harry Potter's headmaster because she pictured him humming to himself.

The money from J. M. Barrie's book *Peter Pan* goes to the Great Ormond Street Hospital for children in London, England.

Teeny Ted from Turnip Town is the world's smallest book. It cost $15,000 (£10,000) to produce and it's so minuscule, it fits on a human hair.

THE BESTSELLING SINGLE-VOLUME BOOK OF ALL TIME IS THE LORD OF THE RINGS (150 MILLION COPIES) BY J. R. R. TOLKIEN.

SIX EDITORS, FIVE DESIGNERS AND MANY LEGO® MINIFIGURES ALL HELPED TO MAKE THIS BOOK.

Fact Attack

John Steinbeck's original manuscript for *Of Mice and Men* was eaten by a dog.

The first US e-book was a copy of the Declaration of Independence.

READ ALL ABOUT IT

Reading makes you cleverer, keeps you sharp and makes you a better writer, too.

You're reading a book about facts. Well, here are some facts about books.

One copy of *The Little*

C. S. Lewis destroyed the first version of *The Lion, the Witch and the Wardrobe* because his friends criticized it.

Charles Dickens built a tunnel from his main house to a little house where he wrote.

Alice in Wonderland has been translated into 176 languages.

A fairy tale about a runaway gingerbreadman was first published in 1875. Sweet!

THE **MOST VALUABLE BOOK** IN THE WORLD IS A COPY OF JOHN JAMES AUDUBON'S *BIRDS OF AMERICA*. IT IS WORTH OVER US **$10 MILLION**.

DR SEUSS'S EDITOR CHALLENGED HIM TO WRITE A BOOK USING ONLY 50 WORDS. THE RESULT WAS *GREEN EGGS AND HAM*.

ROALD DAHL INVENTED ABOUT **250 NEW WORDS**. MOST APPEAR IN *THE BFG*. HIS LANGUAGE IS KNOWN AS GOBBLEFUNK.

Cinderella was first published by French author Charles Perrault in 1697.

Prince was 2 m (6 ft 7 in) tall!

The record for the most people balancing books on their heads was 998 people in 2012.

In 1921 *The Tale of Peter Rabbit*, by Beatrix Potter, was published in braille.

We hope you enjoyed our book!

GLOSSARY

We are a robot army. We can do any job. We are on page 112.

ALGAE
Simple plants that have no true roots or flowers.

ARCHAEOLOGIST
An expert who finds out about human history by digging up things and studying them.

ARCHITECT
A person who designs buildings.

ARTIFICIAL INTELLIGENCE
The science and study of building machines that have the ability to learn and think in human-like ways.

ASTEROID
A rock that floats in space, orbiting the Sun.

ASTRONAUT
A person who has been trained to travel and work in a spacecraft.

ATMOSPHERE
The layer of mixed gases that surrounds a planet.

ATOM
A tiny particle of matter. Atoms are composed of smaller particles: electrons, protons and neutrons.

BLACK HOLE
An area in space where gravity is so strong that nothing can escape it, not even light.

BLUBBER
The layer of fat between the skin and muscle of whales and other animals.

CANYON
A deep valley with steep sides, often with a stream flowing through it.

CARNIVORE
An animal that eats meat.

CARTILAGE
A tough, flexible tissue that covers the ends of bones in joints.

CONSERVATIONIST
Someone who promotes careful management of the natural environment.

CULTURE
The inherited ideas, beliefs, values and knowledge of a group of people.

DRONE
An unmanned aircraft or ship that can navigate without human control or beyond the line of sight.

ELEMENT
A substance that cannot be broken down into simpler ingredients.

EMPIRE
A group of nations that are ruled over by a leader or government.

EXOPLANET
A planet that orbits a star other than the Sun.

FAULT
A line of weakness or a crack in Earth's crust along which a plate of rock can shift or slide.

FOSSIL
The ancient remains of an animal or plant that lived thousands of years ago. A fossil may be animal remains, footprints or a plant, preserved in rock.

GALLEON
A large sailing ship of the 15th to 17th centuries that was used as either a fighting or a merchant ship.

GLADIATOR
A man in ancient Rome who was trained to fight to the death in the arena.

GRAVITY
The force that attracts objects towards one another. It is also the force that attracts, or pulls, objects towards the Earth.

Let's rock! For the music, go to page 158, and for the stony kind, check out page 56.

What's a rain-making laser beam? Find out on page 106.

We will turn the page ...
We will turn the page ...

HUMANOID
Looking like a human being.

INFLATABLE
A small rubber boat that is inflated with air.

LABYRINTH
A maze of paths or passageways in which it is difficult to find one's way or to reach the exit.

LASER
An intense, focused beam of light used for communications, cutting, welding, astronomy, surgery and much more.

MAGNET
A substance or object that attracts certain substances, such as the metal iron.

METEORITE
A rock from space that reaches Earth's surface without burning up in the atmosphere.

NANOBOT
A microscopic robot.

PAPYRUS
A tall water-plant that was used as paper by the ancient Egyptians.

PARTICLE
A tiny part, such as an atom or molecule, that makes up matter.

PHARAOH
The title given to the rulers of ancient Egypt.

PHOTOPHORE
A glowing organ found in certain deep-sea fishes.

PLANETARIUM
A building where the movements of the Sun, Moon, planets and stars are projected on to the inside of a domed ceiling.

PLATEAU
A large area on land or under the sea that is mostly flat, usually with lower areas around it.

PROSPECTING
Searching for gold.

RAINFOREST
A tropical forest with tall, evergreen trees and a high annual rainfall.

RAPTOR
A meat-eating dinosaur that ran on its hind legs.

SAUROPOD
A gentle, plant-eating dinosaur, often very large, with a long neck and a long, whip-like tail.

SEISMIC
Relating to, or caused by, earthquakes or earth tremors.

SPACE JUNK
Objects such as satellites and material discarded or lost from space stations that remain in space after they have been used.

SPECIES
A particular group of living things, whose members look similar and breed together.

SUBMERSIBLE
A ship that submerges and operates underwater.

TOUCHSCREEN
A touch-sensitive display screen on a computer or electronic device.

TSUNAMI
A huge wave produced by a seaquake or undersea volcanic eruption.

Lucky we have a glossary. Even I learned some new words in this book!

OLD TIMES

There's gold on page 32. Take me there and find out who the Aztecs and Incas were.

I'm spelunking on page 94. It's awesome!

INDEX

I need to get this parrot back to the rain forest. Let's find our way back to page 80 ...